500 RECIPES AND HINTS FOR PRESSURE COOKING

by Moya Maynard

HAMLYN
LONDON · NEW YORK · SYDNEY · TORONTO

Contents

The author extends her thanks to the following for their help and advice:

Brown and Polson Information Service
Danepak Ltd
Danish Agricultural Producers
Flour Advisory Bureau
Knorr Information Service
Lea and Perrins Worcestershire Sauce
Pasta Foods Ltd
The Prestige Group Ltd
RHM Foods Ltd
Tower Housewares Ltd
US Rice Council

Published by The Hamlyn Publishing Group Limited
London · New York · Sydney · Toronto
Astronaut House, Feltham, Middlesex, England

© Copyright The Hamlyn Publishing Group Limited 1978

ISBN 0 600 37168 9

Sixth impression 1984

Printed and bound in Great Britain by
R. J. Acford

Useful Facts and Figures

Notes on metrication

In this book quantities are given in metric and Imperial measures. Exact conversion from Imperial to metric measures does not usually give very convenient working quantities and so the metric measures have been rounded off into units of 25 grams. The table below shows the recommended equivalents.

Ounces	Approx g to nearest whole figure	Recommended conversion to nearest unit of 25
1	28	25
2	57	50
3	85	75
4	113	100
5	142	150
6	170	175
7	198	200
8	227	225
9	255	250
10	283	275
11	312	300
12	340	350
13	368	375
14	396	400
15	425	425
16 (1 lb)	454	450
17	482	475
18	510	500
19	539	550
20 (1¼ lb)	567	575

Note:
When converting quantities over 20 oz first add the appropriate figures in the centre column, then adjust to the nearest unit of 25. As a general guide, 1 kg (1000 g) equals 2·2 lb or about 2 lb 3 oz. This method of conversion gives good results in nearly all cases, although in certain pastry and cake recipes a more accurate conversion is necessary to produce a balanced recipe.

Liquid measures: The millilitre has been used in this book and the following table gives a few examples.

Imperial	Approx ml to nearest whole figure	Recommended ml
¼ pint	142	150 ml
½ pint	283	300 ml
¾ pint	425	450 ml
1 pint	567	600 ml
1½ pints	851	900 ml
1¾ pints	992	1000 ml (1 litre)

Spoon measures: All spoon measures given in this book are level unless otherwise stated.

Can sizes: At present, cans are marked with the exact (usually to the nearest whole number) metric equivalent of the Imperial weight of the contents, so we have followed this practice when giving can sizes.

Notes for American and Australian users

In America the 8-oz measuring cup is used. In Australia metric measures are now used in conjunction with the standard 250-ml measuring cup. The Imperial pint, used in Britain and Australia, is 20 fl oz, while the American pint is 16 fl oz. It is important to remember that the Australian tablespoon differs from both the British and American tablespoons; the table below gives a comparison. The British standard tablespoon, which has been used throughout this book, holds 17·7 ml, the American 14·2 ml, and the Australian 20 ml. A teaspoon holds approximately 5 ml in all three countries.

British	American	Australian
1 teaspoon	1 teaspoon	1 teaspoon
1 tablespoon	1 tablespoon	1 tablespoon
2 tablespoons	3 tablespoons	2 tablespoons
3½ tablespoons	4 tablespoons	3 tablespoons
4 tablespoons	5 tablespoons	3½ tablespoons

An Imperial/American guide to solid and liquid measures

Solid measures

IMPERIAL	AMERICAN
1 lb butter or margarine	2 cups
1 lb flour	4 cups
1 lb granulated or castor sugar	2 cups
1 lb icing sugar	3 cups
8 oz rice	1 cup

Liquid measures

IMPERIAL	AMERICAN
¼ pint liquid	⅔ cup liquid
½ pint	1¼ cups
¾ pint	2 cups
1 pint	2½ cups
1½ pints	3¾ cups
2 pints	5 cups (2½ pints)

Note:
When making any of the recipes in this book, only follow one set of measures as they are not interchangeable.

Soups

The basis of a good soup is the stock. With a pressure cooker stock making, which is usually a lengthy process, can be achieved in 40 minutes. Because of this, bones and left-over vegetables need never be wasted and good nutritious meals can be made more economically. If, however, concentrated stock or soup is being made for the freezer, it is essential to use fresh uncooked ingredients. Large quantities can be divided into convenient amounts and frozen in suitable containers.

Home-made stock can enhance and improve a range of dishes, soups, casseroles, sauces and vegetable purées. In this chapter, there is a selection of soups and chowders, some of which can form the main course of a meal.

Hints:
Use the cooker without the trivet.
Sauté vegetables in the open cooker.
Always add thickening agents at the end of cooking.
Pulse soups, or those liquidised, do not generally need a thickening agent.
The cooker should never be more than half full.
Reduce quantity of stock, thinning later to give the required consistency.
Bring to high pressure and reduce pressure at room temperature.
Taste and adjust seasonings after cooking.

Cream of carrot soup

cooking time: 5 minutes
pressure: high

you will need for 4–6 servings:

METRIC/IMPERIAL
1 onion, chopped	strip of lemon peel
25 g/1 oz butter	salt and pepper
575 g/1¼ lb carrots, sliced	¼ teaspoon dried thyme
1 litre/1¾ pints chicken stock	150 ml/¼ pint single cream or milk

1 Place the onion and butter in the cooker with the trivet removed. Cook for 5 minutes to soften the onion without browning.
2 Add the carrots, stock, lemon peel, a little salt, pepper and the thyme.

3 Make sure the cooker is no more than half full, then bring to high pressure and cook for 5 minutes. Reduce pressure at room temperature.
4 Remove ingredients from the cooker and either sieve or blend them in a liquidiser.
5 Reheat the soup in the cooker, stir in the single cream, taste and adjust seasoning before serving.

Brussels sprout soup

cooking time: 5 minutes
pressure: high

you will need for 6 servings:

METRIC/IMPERIAL
450 g/1 lb fresh Brussels sprouts	salt and pepper
	150 ml/¼ pint milk
1 onion, chopped	150 ml/¼ pint single cream
1 litre/1¾ pints chicken stock	

1 Prepare the sprouts and place in the cooker with the trivet removed. Add the onion, stock, salt and pepper. Make sure the cooker is no more than half full.
2 Bring to high pressure and cook for 5 minutes. Reduce pressure at room temperature.
3 Sieve or blend ingredients in a liquidiser.
4 Reheat in the cooker, stirring in the milk and cream. Taste and adjust seasoning.

Spicy lentil soup

cooking time: 10 minutes
pressure: high

you will need for 4–6 servings:

METRIC/IMPERIAL
100 g/4 oz lentils	2 sticks celery, sliced
900 ml/1½ pints ham stock	bay leaf
1 large onion, sliced	½ teaspoon dried thyme
2 carrots, sliced	1 tablespoon paprika

1 Wash the lentils and place in the cooker with the trivet removed.
2 Add the remaining ingredients making sure the cooker is no more than half full. Bring gradually up to high pressure and cook for 10 minutes.
3 Reduce pressure at room temperature.
4 Taste and adjust seasoning; serve the soup with garlic bread.

Smoked fish chowder

cooking time: 5 minutes
pressure: high

you will need for 4–6 servings:

METRIC/IMPERIAL

225 g/8 oz smoked cod fillet	600 ml/1 pint chicken stock
25 g/1 oz butter	175 g/6 oz potato, peeled and diced
1 onion, chopped	300 ml/½ pint milk
1 teaspoon curry powder	

to garnish:
little chopped parsley

1 Wash the fish, remove any bones and skin. Cut into pieces.
2 Melt the butter in the cooker, with the trivet removed, and fry the onion for 2 minutes without browning.
3 Stir in the curry powder, stock and potato, and making sure the cooker is no more than half full, bring to high pressure and cook for 5 minutes. Reduce pressure at room temperature.
4 Stir in the milk, salt if necessary and pepper. Reheat.
5 Serve sprinkled with chopped parsley.

Chicken and vegetable broth

cooking time: 45 minutes
pressure: high

you will need for 6–8 servings:

METRIC/IMPERIAL

1 chicken or capon carcass	2 onions, chopped
1·75 litres/3 pints water	3 large carrots, chopped
salt and pepper	2 sticks celery, sliced
	1 potato, diced

to garnish:
1 tablespoon chopped parsley

1 Break up the carcass and place the pieces with the water in the open cooker with the trivet removed, making sure the cooker is no more than half full. Bring slowly to the boil.
2 Using a slotted spoon, remove the scum that forms on the surface. Add a little salt and pepper.
3 Bring to high pressure and cook for 40 minutes. Allow pressure to reduce at room temperature.
4 Remove the meat from the bones and discard the bones. Add the prepared vegetables to the meat and liquid in the cooker, bring to high pressure and cook for 5 minutes. Allow pressure to reduce at room temperature.
5 Sieve or blend the broth in a liquidiser.
6 Reheat it in the cooker and adjust seasoning. Serve sprinkled with the chopped parsley.

Beetroot soup

cooking time: 5 minutes
pressure: high

you will need for 4–6 servings:

METRIC/IMPERIAL

25 g/1 oz butter	1 litre/1¾ pints beef stock
1 large carrot, finely grated	bay leaf
1 onion, finely grated	1 tablespoon red wine vinegar
100 g/4 oz cabbage, shredded	juice of 1 orange (optional)
450 g/1 lb cooked beetroot	1 teaspoon castor sugar
	salt and pepper

1 Melt the butter in the cooker, with the trivet removed, and sauté the carrot, onion and cabbage.
2 Peel and grate the beetroot and add the remaining ingredients, making sure the cooker is no more than half full.
3 Bring to high pressure and cook for 5 minutes. Reduce pressure at room temperature.
4 Taste the soup and adjust seasoning if necessary. If liked, serve with each bowl a little soured cream.

Oxtail soup

cooking time: 40 minutes
pressure: high

you will need for 4–6 servings:

METRIC/IMPERIAL

1 medium oxtail	bouquet garni
1 tablespoon oil	salt and pepper
2 turnips, chopped	1 litre/2 pints beef stock or water
2 onions, chopped	
2 carrots, chopped	2–3 tablespoons port or Burgundy
1–2 sticks celery, chopped	

This soup should be made the day before it is required, so that the fat may be skimmed from the surface. Ask the butcher to cut the oxtail into joints.
1 Wash and dry the joints. Heat the oil in the open cooker, with the trivet removed, and sauté the joints until browned on all sides.
2 Add the prepared and chopped vegetables, bouquet garni, salt and pepper and stock, making sure that the cooker is not more than half full.
3 Bring to high pressure and cook for 40 minutes. Allow the pressure to reduce at room temperature.
4 Strain the soup and take the meat off the bones. Keep the soup and the meat separately in the refrigerator overnight.
5 The next day, skim the fat from the surface and place the soup and pieces of meat in a pan. Bring to the boil, check the seasoning and stir in the port or Burgundy. Boil for 2–3 minutes, then serve.
6 If a thicker oxtail soup is preferred, whisk in small pieces of beurre manié (equal quantities of butter and flour blended together) before adding the wine.

Cream of vegetable soup

cooking time: 8 minutes
pressure: high

you will need for 6 servings:

METRIC/IMPERIAL
50 g/2 oz butter
225 g/8 oz onion, chopped
225 g/8 oz celery, sliced
450 g/1 lb potatoes, sliced
450 ml/¾ pint chicken
   stock
bay leaf

small clove of garlic,
   crushed
salt and pepper
¼ teaspoon turmeric
   (optional)
150 ml/¼ pint milk
150 ml/¼ pint single cream

to garnish:
chopped parsley

Melt the butter in the cooker with the trivet removed.
Add the onions, celery and potatoes, stir round and
cook for 2 minutes.
Stir in the stock, bay leaf, garlic, salt and pepper and
turmeric if used.
Making sure the cooker is no more than half full,
bring to high pressure and cook for 8 minutes.
Reduce pressure at room temperature.
Blend the milk and cream together and stir into the
soup.
Heat through and serve sprinkled with a little
chopped parsley.

Quick vegetable soup

cooking time: 5 minutes
pressure: high

you will need for 4 servings:

METRIC/IMPERIAL
2 rashers streaky bacon
1 tablespoon oil
1 large onion, chopped
2 carrots, chopped
100 g/4 oz potatoes, diced
100 g/4 oz leeks, or
   turnip, sliced or diced

1 (397-g/14-oz) can
   tomatoes
300 ml/½ pint beef stock
salt and pepper

Remove rind from the bacon, cut into pieces.
Place bacon, oil and onion in the base of the cooker,
with the trivet removed, and cook gently for 2
minutes.
Stir in the remaining ingredients, making sure the
cooker is no more than half full.
Bring to high pressure and cook for 5 minutes.
Reduce pressure at room temperature.
Serve sprinkled with grated cheese and French
bread.

Variations:
Use celery instead of leek or turnip.
Omit bacon and use Marmite for the stock to make
a vegetarian soup.

c Add a few fresh herbs to give an extra special
flavour.

⬤ Hint:
The vegetables should be cut to roughly the same
size or they will not cook evenly.

Scotch broth

cooking time: 23 minutes
pressure: high

you will need for 6–8 servings:

METRIC/IMPERIAL
2 breasts of lamb
50 g/2 oz pearl barley
175 g/6 oz onions,
   chopped
225 g/8 oz carrots, sliced

175 g/6 oz turnips, diced
2 leeks, sliced
salt and pepper
bouquet garni

to garnish:
parsley, finely chopped

1 Cut the breast of lamb into pieces and place in the
cooker with the trivet removed. Pour in 1·5 litres/2½
pints water, making sure the cooker is no more than
half full.
2 Cover, bring to high pressure and cook for 15
minutes. Reduce pressure at room temperature.
3 Lift out the lamb, save the meat and discard the fat
and bones. Strain the stock and leave it to become
cold so that the fat hardens.
4 Place the pearl barley in a saucepan, bring to the
boil and cook for 5 minutes, then drain.
5 Remove and discard the fat from the stock. Cut the
meat into pieces. Put the prepared meat, barley and
remaining ingredients in the cooker with the stock.
6 Bring to high pressure and cook for 7 minutes.
Reduce pressure at room temperature.
7 Serve sprinkled with chopped parsley.

Chilled leek and tomato soup

cooking time: 5 minutes
pressure: high

you will need for 4 servings:

METRIC/IMPERIAL
2 medium leeks
15 g/½ oz butter
225 g/8 oz tomatoes, cut
   into quarters
300 ml/½ pint chicken
   stock

½ teaspoon chicken stock
   powder
salt and pepper
300 ml/½ pint milk

to garnish:
freshly chopped chives

1 Trim off some of the green leaves and thoroughly
wash the leeks to remove grit. Cut into rings.
2 Melt the butter in the cooker with the trivet removed,

add the leeks, stir round and cook for 2 minutes.

3 Add the tomatoes, stock and stock powder, salt and pepper. Bring to high pressure and cook for 5 minutes. Reduce pressure at room temperature.
4 Either sieve or liquidise the vegetables, stir in the milk, taste and adjust seasonings.
5 Chill well before serving and sprinkle with chopped chives.

Carrot and apricot soup

cooking time: 10 minutes
pressure: high

you will need for 4–6 servings:

METRIC/IMPERIAL	
15 g/½ oz butter or margarine	100 g/4 oz tomatoes, quartered
1 large onion, chopped	450 ml/¾ pint chicken stock, or water with 1 stock cube
2 carrots, sliced	
100 g/4 oz potatoes, diced	¼ teaspoon dried thyme
100 g/4 oz fresh apricots, halved and with stones removed	bay leaf
	salt and pepper

1 Melt the butter or margarine in the cooker with the trivet removed, add the onion and cook gently for a few minutes to soften slightly.
2 Add the remaining ingredients, making sure the cooker is no more than half full.
3 Bring to high pressure and cook for 10 minutes. Reduce pressure at room temperature.
4 Sieve or liquidise the soup to make a purée.
5 Reheat, taste and adjust seasonings. For serving, sprinkle with a little chopped parsley.

Corn and ham chowder

cooking time: 15 minutes and 10 minutes
pressure: high

you will need for 6 servings:

METRIC/IMPERIAL	
1 forehock bacon shank	pepper
225 g/8 oz onion, sliced	2 tablespoons flour
350 g/12 oz potatoes, diced	chopped parsley
1 (326-g/11½-oz) can sweet corn	

1 Place the shank in the cooker, with the trivet removed, and cover it with cold water. Bring slowly to the boil in the open cooker. Remove from heat and pour off the water.
2 Pour 1 litre/1¾ pints fresh water into the cooker with the shank. Bring to high pressure and cook for 15 minutes. Reduce pressure at room temperature.
3 When cool enough to handle remove the rind from the shank. Cut the meat into pieces and return to the

cooker with the bone. Add the onions, potatoes, sweet corn and pepper, making sure the cooker is no more than half full.
4 Bring to high pressure and cook for 10 minutes. Reduce pressure at room temperature. Remove the bone.
5 Blend the flour with a little water, add some of the hot liquor, return to the cooker and bring to the boil, stirring well for a few minutes to thicken.
6 Stir in the parsley, taste, and adjust seasoning if necessary. Serve with chunks of bread.

Variation:
If liked, creamed sweet corn could be used. This should be stirred in at the time of thickening.

Split pea soup with frankfurters

cooking time: 12 minutes
pressure: high

you will need for 4–6 servings:

METRIC/IMPERIAL	
4 rashers streaky bacon, chopped	bouquet garni
1 small onion, chopped	¼ teaspoon dried thyme
1 litre/1¾ pints water	salt and pepper
100 g/4 oz split peas	4–8 frankfurters

1 Gently fry the bacon in the cooker, with the trivet removed, until the fat runs. Add the onion, and cook for 5 minutes without colouring.
2 Add the water, peas, bouquet garni and a little salt and pepper. Stir well. Make sure the cooker is no more than half full.
3 Bring to high pressure and cook for 12 minutes. Allow pressure to reduce at room temperature.
4 Remove bouquet garni, then either sieve or pass the soup through a liquidiser to make a smooth purée. Rinse the cooker, return the purée and add sliced frankfurters.
5 Bring to the boil, stirring, and simmer gently for 5 minutes to heat the frankfurters. Serve with crisp French bread.

Split pea and celery soup

cooking time: 10 minutes
pressure: high

you will need for 4 servings:

METRIC/IMPERIAL	
225 g/8 oz green split peas	1 litre/1¾ pints chicken stock
225 g/8 oz celery, washed and sliced	½ teaspoon dried mixed herbs
350 g/12 oz onions, chopped	150 ml/¼ pint milk
	salt and pepper

1 Wash the peas, drain them and put them in the cooker, with the trivet removed. Add the celery, onions and stock.
2 Bring to high pressure and cook for 10 minutes. Reduce pressure at room temperature.
3 Sieve or liquidise the ingredients for a smooth consistency. Return them to the cooker, add herbs, milk, salt and pepper to taste.
4 Heat gently for serving immediately and serve with fried croûtons.

Variations:

a If liked, a ham bone could be used for extra flavour.
b Fry the croûtons in garlic butter.
c For a change, serve with a spoonful of garlic cream cheese on top of each portion.

Chicken and rice soup

cooking time: 8 minutes and 5 minutes
pressure: high

you will need for 4–5 servings:

METRIC/IMPERIAL

I chicken carcass	I litre/1¾ pints water
½ teaspoon dried mixed herbs	75 g/3 oz long-grain rice
I large onion, chopped	225 g/8 oz sweet corn kernels
I carrot, sliced	salt and pepper

1 Place chicken carcass, herbs, onion, carrot and water in the cooker, with the trivet removed.
2 Bring to high pressure, making sure the cooker is no more than half full, and cook for 8 minutes. Reduce pressure at room temperature.
3 Strain, take the chicken meat off the bones and return it with the stock to the cooker. Add the rice and corn.
4 Bring to the boil and stir once. Return to high pressure and cook for 5 minutes. Reduce pressure with cold water.
5 Check seasoning and serve with croûtons.

Carrot and parsnip soup

cooking time: 10 minutes
pressure: high

you will need for 4–6 servings:

METRIC/IMPERIAL

25 g/I oz butter	I litre/1¾ pints stock
I small onion, chopped	salt and pepper
350 g/12 oz parsnips, peeled and sliced	½ teaspoon dried basil
450 g/I lb carrots, peeled and sliced	300 ml/½ pint milk

1 Heat the butter in the cooker, with the trivet removed, add the onion, parsnips and carrots, stir round and cook for 3 minutes.

2 Add the stock, salt, pepper and basil.
3 Bring to high pressure and cook for 10 minutes, making sure the cooker is no more than half full. Reduce pressure at room temperature.
4 Sieve or liquidise the soup.
5 Return to the cooker, stir in the milk, taste and adjust seasonings, reheat for serving.

French onion soup

cooking time: 4 minutes
pressure: high

you will need for 4 servings:

METRIC/IMPERIAL

½ kg/I lb onions	bay leaf
50 g/2 oz butter	few drops Worcestershire sauce or I tablespoon Madeira per serving
I litre/1¾ pints stock made with 2 beef stock cubes	4 slices French bread
salt and pepper	

to garnish:
100 g/4 oz Gruyère or Cheddar cheese, grated

1 Peel and thinly slice the onions. Heat the butter in the open cooker, with the trivet removed, and sauté the onions over a very low heat for 10 minutes until they are softened and just beginning to brown.
2 Add the stock, seasoning and bay leaf, making sure that the cooker is no more than half full. Bring to high pressure and cook for 4 minutes. Allow the pressure to reduce at room temperature.
3 Remove the bay leaf, then ladle the soup into four flameproof bowls. Stir either a few drops of Worcestershire sauce or 1 tablespoon Madeira into each bowl of soup, then add a slice of French bread.
4 Sprinkle the bread with a generous amount of grated cheese, then put the bowls of soup under a preheated grill for 2–3 minutes until the cheese is bubbling.
5 Serve garnished with chopped parsley.

● **Hint:**
To obtain a good, rich flavour to this soup it is important that the onions should be sautéed very slowly.

Pâtés and Meat Loaves

Once you have mastered the art of using a pressure cooker, you will be surprised at the variety of dishes that can be cooked in this way.

Pâtés and meat loaves come into this category. The cooking time is very much reduced, saving fuel, and there is no need to heat an oven, as frequently happens, to cook the one dish only.

The principle of cooking a pâté is to keep it moist, which is usually done in a bain-marie in the oven. With a pressure cooker the same principle is applied, as the container is surrounded by water.

● **Hints:**

a First check that the intended container will fit into the cooker, making sure that the cooker will not be more than half full.

b The container must be well covered and tied securely to make it watertight.

c Favourite recipes can be used, but remember to add a little less liquid as there is not so much dehydration because of the shorter cooking time.

Pork pâté

cooking time: 20 minutes
pressure: high

you will need for 8–10 servings:

METRIC/IMPERIAL

350 g/12 oz pig's liver	½ teaspoon garlic salt
225 g/8 oz streaky bacon rashers	freshly ground pepper
350 g/12 oz pork sausage-meat	1 teaspoon Worcestershire sauce
	25 g/1 oz stuffed olives

1 Trim the pig's liver, cover with milk and leave for 30 minutes. Remove rind and any bone from the bacon.

2 Using half the best-looking rashers, spread and lengthen them with the back of a knife and use them to line a 1-litre/1¾-pint plastic or china pudding basin.

3 Dry the liver on kitchen paper and with the rest of the bacon put it through the mincer. Place the minced liver and bacon in a bowl, add the sausage-meat, garlic salt, pepper, Worcestershire sauce and mix well together.

4 Transfer the mixture to the bacon-lined bowl and press in the olives at intervals and at different levels. Fold over any extra ends of bacon, cover bowl with a double layer of greaseproof paper or foil.

5 Pour 600 ml/1 pint water into the cooker and place the bowl on the trivet, making sure the cooker is not more than half full. Bring to high pressure and cook for 20 minutes. Reduce pressure at room temperature, remove bowl, drain off the fat and allow the pâté to become cold.

6 Turn out by loosening carefully with a knife.

to freeze:

Allow to cool completely, either freeze as a whole pâté or cut in half or wedges and wrap in two layers of freezer packaging to prevent transference of flavour.

Pork and veal pâté

cooking time: 20 minutes
pressure: high

you will need for 8 servings:

METRIC/IMPERIAL

450 g/1 lb lean belly of pork	salt and pepper
350 g/12 oz pig's liver	1 teaspoon dried sage
225 g/8 oz lean pie veal	2 tablespoons stock
1 small onion	100 g/4 oz streaky bacon
1 small cooking apple, peeled and quartered	

1 Trim the belly of pork. Mince it with the liver, veal, onion and apple. Mix together, add salt and pepper, sage and the stock.

2 Remove the rind from the bacon rashers and stretch them with the back of a knife.

3 Line a 1-litre/2-pint heatproof container or tin which will fit into the cooker, with the bacon rashers. Put the minced mixture into the container and level the surface. Cover with double greaseproof paper or foil and tie down.

4 Put 1 litre/1¾ pints water in the cooker and place the container on the trivet. Bring to high pressure and cook for 20 minutes.

5 Reduce pressure at room temperature and leave the pâté to become cold.

To freeze:

Turn out of tin when cold. If liked, cut into slices, wrap in foil and freeze for up to 3 months. Thaw at room temperature.

Veal, ham and egg loaf

cooking time: 35 minutes
pressure: high

you will need for 6–8 servings:

METRIC/IMPERIAL
350 g/12 oz minced veal
100 g/4 oz cooked ham, minced
1 onion, minced
100 g/4 oz fresh bread-crumbs
½ lemon, grated
½ teaspoon dried sage
1 egg, well beaten
1 tablespoon chopped parsley
salt and freshly ground pepper
2 hard-boiled eggs, shelled

1 Mix the veal, ham, onion, breadcrumbs, lemon, sage, egg and parsley together, add salt and pepper.
2 Put half the mixture in a 450-g/1-lb loaf tin, place the whole eggs along the centre and cover the eggs completely with the remaining meat mixture. Level the surface.
3 Cover with double greaseproof paper and foil: seal securely.
4 Pour 600 ml/1 pint water into the cooker, place the loaf tin on the trivet. Bring to high pressure and cook for 35 minutes. Reduce pressure at room temperature.
5 Press the loaf lightly to avoid squashing the eggs, and allow to cool.

5 Remove core and peel from apple. Cut apple into thin slices and toss in lemon juice.
6 Arrange slices overlapping along top of the loaf and garnish dish with parsley sprigs.

Beef and liver loaf

cooking time: 20 minutes
pressure: high

you will need for 4 servings:

METRIC/IMPERIAL
100 g/4 oz lamb's liver
1 large onion
1 large egg
350 g/12 oz minced beef
1 teaspoon dried mixed herbs
1 teaspoon salt
pepper
1 teaspoon Worcestershire sauce

1 Mince the liver and onion and mix with the remaining ingredients.
2 Place in a 600-ml/1-pint dish that will fit into the cooker, cover with foil and tie down.
3 Put 600 ml/1 pint water in the cooker and place dish on the trivet. Bring to high pressure and cook for 20 minutes. Reduce pressure at room temperature.
4 Serve either hot or cold.

Apple and sausage meat loaf

cooking time: 25 minutes
pressure: high

you will need for 6–8 servings:

METRIC/IMPERIAL
675 g/1½ lb sausage meat
350 g/12 oz cooking apples, peeled and grated
1 large onion, peeled and grated

to garnish:
1 small dessert apple
2 teaspoons lemon juice

50 g/2 oz fresh white breadcrumbs
2 tablespoons Worcestershire sauce
4 slices (about 100 g/4 oz) cooked ham

sprigs of parsley

1 Mix thoroughly all ingredients, except ham slices. Line the bottom and sides of a 1-kg/2-lb loaf tin with ham slices. Do not trim slices if they are too big.
2 Fill tin with the meat mixture and fold over ham slices. Cover with foil and roll under the rim of the tin to secure.
3 Pour 450 ml/¾ pint water into the cooker and place the tin on the trivet. Bring to high pressure and cook for 25 minutes. Reduce pressure at room temperature.
4 Allow the loaf to cool completely in the tin before turning out.

Beef galantine

cooking time: 40 minutes
pressure: high

you will need for 6–8 servings:

METRIC/IMPERIAL
100 g/4 oz fresh bread-crumbs
100 g/4 oz mushrooms, chopped
450 g/1 lb fresh beef mince
225 g/8 oz grated carrot
1 onion, grated
6 olives, chopped
1 tablespoon Worcestershire sauce
1 tablespoon tomato purée
1 teaspoon dried mixed herbs
1 tablespoon chopped parsley
1 large egg, well beaten
salt and pepper

1 Line the base of a 15-cm/6-inch cake tin with grease-proof paper.
2 Mix all the ingredients together and place in the prepared tin. Level the surface, cover with a piece of greaseproof and foil and tie down securely.
3 Fill the cooker with 600 ml/1 pint water and place the tin on the trivet.
4 Bring to high pressure and cook for 40 minutes. Reduce pressure at room temperature and allow to cool before turning out.

Chicken pâté

cooking time: 20 minutes
pressure: high

you will need for 4 servings:

METRIC/IMPERIAL

2 rashers streaky bacon
1 large onion, chopped
225 g/8 oz chicken livers
6 tablespoons boiling
  water

1 small clove garlic, peeled
225 g/8 oz cooked chicken
1 chicken stock cube
3 large eggs, well beaten
salt and pepper

to garnish:
1 tablespoon chopped
  parsley

1 Remove the rind and chop the bacon. Place the bacon and onion in a frying pan and cook slowly for about 10 minutes to extract the fat.
2 Trim the livers and add to the pan: stir round and cook for 5 minutes.
3 Mince the bacon, onion, livers, garlic and chicken. Dissolve the stock cube in the boiling water, and add the minced meats with the remaining ingredients.
4 Put the mixture into a 1½-pint soufflé dish that will fit into the cooker. Cover with double greaseproof paper and tie down.
5 Pour 600 ml/1 pint water into the cooker, and place dish on the trivet. Bring to high pressure and cook for 20 minutes. Reduce pressure at room temperature, and leave the pâté in the dish to become firm.
6 Serve slightly chilled, garnished with parsley.

Fish

It should not be forgotten that fish can be cooked in a pressure cooker, although the cooking time is only short. It is a particularly good way of cooking fish for invalids and people on special diets. There is also a great reduction in the characteristic fish-cooking smells.

Less liquid is needed than with traditional cooking methods, which means more concentrated flavour and flesh which is not so likely to break up.

Herby haddock

cooking time: 6 minutes
pressure: high

you will need for 4 servings:

METRIC/IMPERIAL
450 g/1 lb fresh haddock fillet
25 g/1 oz cornflour
1 mixed herb stock cube, dissolved in 300 ml/½ pint hot water

1 kg/2 lb potatoes, peeled
3 tablespoons cream or top of the milk

to garnish:
chopped parsley

Skin and bone the fish and cut into cubes. Toss in cornflour.
Melt the butter in the cooker with the trivet removed and sauté the fish until slightly browned.
Add the remaining cornflour to the pan with the stock and bring to the boil, stirring all the time. Put in the potatoes, cut into even-sized pieces.
Make sure the cooker is no more than half full, then bring to high pressure and cook for 6 minutes. Reduce pressure with cold water.
Remove the lid and stir in the cream before serving. Garnish with chopped parsley.

Cod cutlets Parmesan

cooking time: 7 minutes
presssure: high

you will need for 4 servings:

METRIC/IMPERIAL
4 cod cutlets
1 onion, thinly sliced
2 carrots, cut into matchsticks

150 ml/¼ pint water
1 packet Parmesan cheese sauce mix (20 g/¾ oz)
150 ml/¼ pint milk

1 Place the cod cutlets, onion and carrot in the cooker with the trivet removed, add the water.
2 Bring to high pressure and cook for 7 minutes. Reduce pressure with cold water, lift cod cutlets onto the serving dish and keep warm.
3 Blend the Parmesan cheese sauce mix with the milk and stir into the cooker. Bring to the boil, stirring all the time, and simmer for 3 minutes.
4 Pour over the fish to serve.

Soused herrings

cooking time: 6 minutes
pressure: high

you will need for 6 servings:

METRIC/IMPERIAL
6 herrings
salt and pepper
blade mace
2–3 cloves
6 peppercorns
3–4 whole allspice

1 onion, sliced
2 bay leaves
150 ml/¼ pint malt vinegar
150 ml/¼ pint water

Soused herrings may be served as a starter or a main course.
1 Clean the herrings and remove the heads and tails. Split and bone them.
2 Season each fillet with salt and pepper and roll them up from the tail end with the skin outside. Secure with a wooden cocktail stick, and place them in the cooker with the trivet removed.
3 Add the mace, cloves, peppercorns, allspice, onion, bay leaves, vinegar and water. Bring to high pressure and cook for 6 minutes.
4 Reduce the pressure with cold water. Allow the herrings to cool in the cooking liquor.
Serve cold with a selection of salads.

Variations:
a Use orange juice instead of water.
b If liked, sprinkle with a few herbs.

Lemon halibut steaks

cooking time: 4 minutes
pressure: high

you will need for 4 servings:

METRIC/IMPERIAL
50 g/2 oz softened butter
grated rind and juice of ½ lemon
1 tablespoon chopped chives or parsley

salt and pepper
3 evenly thick halibut steaks

1 Cream the butter with the lemon rind and juice, chives or parsley, salt and pepper.
2 Wash and dry the halibut steaks, place on a sheet of foil. Spread the lemon butter over the steaks, and form them into a parcel.
3 Pour 300 ml/½ pint water into the cooker, place the foil parcel on the trivet, bring to high pressure and cook for 4 minutes. Reduce pressure with cold water.
4 Serve at once with mashed potatoes and peas.

Cod niçoise

cooking time: 4 minutes
pressure: high

you will need for 4 servings:

METRIC/IMPERIAL

3 tablespoons oil	½ teaspoon dried basil
2 onions, sliced	50 g/2 oz black olives
I leek, washed and sliced	4 frozen cod steaks cut
2 cloves garlic, crushed	into large cubes
I (397-g/14-oz) can	150 ml/¼ pint water
tomatoes	salt and pepper
225 g/8 oz potatoes, cut	
in I-cm/½-inch slices	

to garnish:

anchovies (optional)	chopped parsley

1 Heat the oil in the cooker with the trivet removed.
2 Put in the onions, leeks and garlic. Stir round and cook for 2 minutes. Add the remaining ingredients.
3 Bring to high pressure and cook for 4 minutes. Reduce pressure with cold water.
4 Arrange in a heated dish, with a lattice of anchovies over the top if liked, and sprinkle with parsley.

Haddock mould

cooking time: 8 minutes
pressure: high

you will need for 4–6 servings:

METRIC/IMPERIAL

575 g/1¼ lb haddock fillets	salt and pepper
25 g/1 oz butter or	I tablespoon chopped
margarine	parsley
I small onion, finely	I teaspoon lemon juice or
chopped	anchovy essence
25 g/1 oz plain flour	2 eggs, well beaten
300 ml/½ pint milk	

1 Skin the fish, remove any obvious bones and chop the flesh.
2 Melt the butter or margarine in a saucepan. Put in the onion and cook slowly without browning.
3 Stir in the flour, cook for 1 minute: gradually add

the milk, beating well to remove any lumps. Bring to the boil and cook for 2 minutes to thicken.
4 Remove pan from the heat, stir in the fish and remaining ingredients.
5 Place this mixture evenly in a 550-ml/1-pint ring mould. Cover with double greaseproof or foil, seal securely.
6 Fill cooker with 300 ml/½ pint water, place mould on the trivet. Bring to high pressure and cook for 8 minutes. Reduce pressure with cold water.
7 Turn out and serve, fill centre with peas and accompany with a tomato sauce.

Variation:
Use smoked haddock as an alternative and serve with rice and a light curry sauce.

Cod duglére

cooking time: 4 minutes
pressure: high

you will need for 4 servings:

METRIC/IMPERIAL

40 g/1½ oz butter or	salt and pepper
margarine	150 ml/¼ pint dry white
I onion, sliced	wine
225 g/8 oz tomatoes,	4 cod steaks
peeled and chopped	
I tablespoon chopped	
parsley	

1 Melt the butter or margarine in the cooker with the trivet removed, add the onion and cook gently for 5 minutes without browning.
2 Add the tomatoes, parsley, salt and pepper, and the wine. Arrange the cod steaks on top.
3 Bring to high pressure and cook for 4 minutes. Reduce pressure with cold water.
4 Serve with mashed potato.

Halibut surprise

cooking time: 4 minutes
pressure: high

you will need for 4 servings:

METRIC/IMPERIAL

4 halibut steaks (about	100 g/4 oz mushrooms,
175-g/6-oz portions)	sliced
2 tablespoons oil	2 tablespoons dry white
3 rashers streaky bacon,	wine
chopped	salt and pepper
225 g/8 oz tomatoes,	
skinned and deseeded	

to garnish:
chopped parsley

1 Wipe the halibut steaks and place each in the centre of a piece of foil large enough to enclose the fish completely.
2 Heat the oil in a frying pan, add the onion and cook until soft, about 5 minutes. Add the bacon, the tomatoes, chopped, and the mushrooms: cook for about 2 minutes.
3 Stir in the wine, salt and pepper and cook to allow the wine to evaporate. Allow to cool a little. Divide this mixture between the halibut steaks, seal each to form a parcel.
4 Pour 300 ml/½ pint water into the cooker: place the parcels on the trivet. Bring to high pressure and cook for 4 minutes. Reduce pressure with cold water.
5 Remove fish from the foil and sprinkle with chopped parsley.

Variations:

a Use capers instead of mushrooms on the fish.
b Chopped anchovies instead of bacon and mushrooms, and a few chopped black olives would be different.
c Lemon juice could be used instead of wine.

Hint

Potatoes and beans could be cooked in the cooker at the same time

Cod portuguaise

cooking time: 4 minutes
pressure: high

you will need for 4 servings:

METRIC/IMPERIAL

100 g/4 oz streaky bacon	2 tablespoons tomato purée
15 g/½ oz butter or margarine	½ teaspoon dried oregano
1 medium onion, chopped	salt and pepper
1 stick celery, sliced	pinch sugar
225 g/8 oz tomatoes, skinned and chopped	4 cod steaks
1 small clove garlic, crushed	

1 Remove rind and chop the bacon: cook gently in a saucepan with the butter or margarine.
2 Add the onion and celery, cook for 3 minutes to soften. Add the tomatoes, garlic if liked, the tomato purée, oregano, salt, pepper and a pinch of sugar.
3 Place the cod steaks on a fairly large piece of foil and spoon the sauce equally over each. Fold the foil into a parcel.
4 Pour 300 ml/½ pint water into the cooker, put the foil parcel on the trivet. Bring to high pressure and cook for 4 minutes. Reduce pressure with cold water.
5 Serve with mashed potatoes. These can have been cooked in the separator at the same time.

Cod with mushrooms and peppers

cooking time: 4 minutes
pressure: high

you will need for 4 servings:

METRIC/IMPERIAL

4 frozen cod steaks	1 medium green pepper
salt and pepper	juice of 1 lemon
100 g/4 oz button mushrooms, washed	

1 Place the cod steaks on a large piece of foil, season with salt and pepper.
2 Slice the mushrooms, wash and deseed the pepper, chop the flesh.
3 Divide these ingredients between the cod steaks. Sprinkle with the lemon juice and seal up the foil like a parcel.
4 Pour 300 ml/½ pint water into the cooker, put the foil parcel on the trivet.
Bring to high pressure and cook for 4 minutes. Reduce pressure at room temperature.
5 Carefully unfold the foil and transfer the cod steaks to a heated serving dish. Serve with mashed potato and sweet corn.

Cod cutlets creole

cooking time: 5 minutes
pressure: high

you will need for 4 servings:

METRIC/IMPERIAL

1 large onion, chopped	6 tomatoes, peeled and finely chopped
1 clove garlic, crushed	150 ml/¼ pint white wine
225 g/8 oz American long-grain rice	450 ml/¾ pint stock
1 tablespoon chopped parsley	4 cod cutlets
75 g/3 oz butter	salt and pepper

1 Place the onion, garlic, rice, parsley and butter in the cooker with the trivet removed. Fry gently until the rice is transparent looking and a golden colour.
2 Add the tomatoes, wine and stock and stir well. Place the cutlets on top and season. Bring to high pressure and cook for 5 minutes. Reduce pressure at room temperature.
3 Serve with the fish in the centre and the rice arranged at each side.

Mackerel with lemon rice stuffing

cooking time: 5 minutes
pressure: high

you will need for 4 servings:

METRIC/IMPERIAL

4 fresh mackerel
175 g/6 oz cooked, long-grain rice (50 g/2 oz uncooked rice: 150 ml/¼ pint stock)
2 sticks celery, finely chopped

rind and juice of 1 lemon
black pepper
1 small egg, beaten
salt

1 Slit the fish open along the vent. Clean and remove backbone from the mackerel.
2 Stuff with cooked rice, celery, lemon rind and juice and black pepper mixed together. Bind with the beaten egg.
3 Close the fish and secure with wooden cocktail sticks. Season the outside of the fish, place in buttered foil and fold to make a parcel.
4 Pour 300 ml/½ pint water into the cooker, place foil parcel on the trivet. Bring to high pressure and cook for 5 minutes.
5 Reduce pressure quickly with cold water.
6 Serve the mackerel in the foil packages.

● **Hint:**
Additional vegetables may be cooked at the same time by using the separator and placing it on top of the fish.

Main Course Dishes

Pot roasts

This is a useful way of cooking whole joints of meat or poultry. The meat is browned in dripping in the open cooker with the trivet removed. Stock should be added and the meat cooked on the trivet. Vegetables may be added 5 minutes before the end of the cooking time and the juices can be thickened and made into gravy. Meat should be even in thickness and not more than 1·5 kg/3 lb in weight.

This is a particularly good way of cooking the cheaper, tougher cuts of meat that have plenty of flavour.

Pressure cooking times to allow per half kilo/per lb for joints of meat

Suitable joints	Cooking time per half kilo/per lb
Beef	
Rolled sirloin	10 minutes
Topside	12 minutes
Rolled rump	10 minutes
Brisket	12 minutes
Silverside	15 minutes
Lamb	
Leg	15 minutes
Breast (boned and rolled)	12 minutes
Pork	
Loin (boned and rolled)	15 minutes
Fillet	12 minutes
Shoulder	15 minutes
Veal	
Fillet	12 minutes
Loin	12 minutes
Shoulder (boned)	14 minutes
Breast (boned and rolled)	14 minutes
Knuckle	10 minutes
Bacon joints	12 minutes
Ox tongue	15 minutes
Frozen joints (unthawed)	25 minutes

Joints for pressure cooking should not weigh more than 1·5 kg/3 lb.

To calculate the amount of liquid required when cooking joints under pressure;
Allow 300 ml/½ pint for first 15 minutes cooking time plus 150 ml/¼ pint for every extra 15 minutes cooking time
e.g. Joint (sirloin) weighs 1·25 kg/2½ lb
    Cooking time = 25 minutes
    Liquid = 450 ml/¾ pint

Pot roast of beef

cooking time: 34 minutes
pressure: high

you will need for 6–8 servings:

METRIC/IMPERIAL
1·5-kg/3-lb piece beef	2 sticks celery, chopped
3 tablespoons pure corn oil	small turnip, diced
1 onion, roughly chopped	3 teaspoons beef stock powder
3 carrots, roughly chopped	450 ml/¾ pint water

1 Tie the beef into a good shape if necessary.
2 Heat the oil in the cooker with the trivet removed and brown the meat on all sides. Remove onto a plate. Brown the onions.
3 Sprinkle in the beef stock powder, add the water and replace the beef.
4 Making sure the cooker is no more than half full, bring to high pressure and cook for 30 minutes. Reduce pressure at room temperature and add the vegetables.
5 Return to high pressure and cook for 4 minutes: reduce at room temperature.
6 Serve the meat sliced with the vegetables and gravy.

Marinaded lamb

cooking time: 30 minutes
pressure: high

you will need for 6–8 servings:

METRIC/IMPERIAL
for the marinade:
1 onion, sliced	150 ml/¼ pint stock
1 carrot, sliced	salt and pepper
1 stick celery, sliced	1 small leg of lamb, boned, weighing not more than 1·5 kg/3 lb
2 sprigs of rosemary	
bay leaf	
½ bottle red wine	
150 ml/¼ pint red wine vinegar	

to cook:
150 ml/¼ pint stock	2 tablespoons plain flour

1 Place the marinade ingredients in the cooker with the trivet removed. Bring to high pressure and cook for 5 minutes: reduce pressure at room temperature and leave to become cold.
2 Place the lamb in a bowl, cover with the marinade and leave for 24 hours, turning once.
3 Drain off all but 300 ml/½ pint of the marinade and stock. Put the joint in the cooker, bring to high pressure and cook for 30 minutes. Reduce pressure at room temperature.
4 Remove the joint on to a serving dish and keep hot. Blend the flour with a little of the stock to remove the lumps, then add the remainder. Pour it back into cooker with the redcurrant jelly, salt and pepper.
5 Bring to the boil stirring, cook for 2 minutes. Strain if necessary and serve with the meat.

Bacon pot roast

cooking time: 12 minutes per half kilo/per lb
pressure: high

you will need for 6–8 servings:

METRIC/IMPERIAL

1·25-kg/2¾-lb unsmoked collar joint	2 tablespoons Worcestershire sauce
450 g/1 lb carrots, quartered lengthways	575 g/1¼ lb potatoes, peeled
2 medium onions, quartered	

1 With the trivet removed, cover the joint with cold water and bring it slowly to the boil in the open cooker.
2 Throw the water away, place the joint on the trivet and pour 450 ml/¾ pint fresh water into the cooker. Add the carrots, onion and Worcestershire sauce.
3 Bring to high pressure and cook for 30 minutes. Reduce pressure with cold water.
4 Cut the potatoes into quarters and place them round the bacon in the stock. Return to high pressure and cook for a further 5 minutes.
5 Reduce pressure with cold water, remove rind from bacon, and serve with the vegetables and cooking liquor.

Devilled shoulder of lamb

cooking time: 12–15 minutes per half kilo/per lb
pressure: high

you will need for 4–6 servings:

METRIC/IMPERIAL

1-kg/2-lb shoulder or leg of lamb	salt and pepper
1 medium onion, chopped	2 teaspoons Worcestershire sauce
2 teaspoons made mustard	450 ml/¾ pint stock
4 tablespoons redcurrant jelly	1 tablespoon plain flour

1 Place the lamb in the cooker with the trivet removed

and fry all over slowly to extract some of the fat. Lift out and keep on one side.
2 Add the onion to the cooker and fry until lightly browned. Add the mustard, redcurrant jelly, salt and pepper, Worcestershire sauce and stock: stir round to dissolve the redcurrant jelly.
3 Return the joint to the cooker. Bring to high pressure and cook for the calculated time. Reduce pressure at room temperature. Remove lamb on to a serving dish and keep hot.
4 Blend the flour with a little water, add some of the hot liquor, return to the cooker. Bring to the boil, stirring: cook for 1 minute.
5 Serve the sauce separately.

Casseroled leg of lamb Provence

cooking time: 12 minutes per half kilo/per lb
pressure: high

you will need for 6 servings:

METRIC/IMPERIAL

1·25-kg/2¾-lb leg of lamb	bay leaf
1 tablespoon oil	salt and pepper
1 large onion, cut into sections	1 green pepper, diced
300 ml/½ pint dry white wine	4 tomatoes, skinned and quartered
150 ml/¼ pint stock	50 g/2 oz stuffed olives
	1 tablespoon cornflour

1 Place the lamb, oil and onion in the cooker with the trivet removed and brown all over. Add the wine, stock, bay leaf, salt and pepper.
2 Bring to high pressure and cook for the calculated time. Reduce pressure at room temperature. Remove the lamb on to a heated serving dish, keep hot.
3 Add the peppers, tomatoes and olives to the cooking liquid and simmer in the open cooker for a few minutes to just soften the vegetables.
4 Blend the cornflour with a little water, add some of the hot stock, return to the cooker and cook for a minute, stirring until thickened.
5 Serve as a thick vegetable sauce in a dish with a spoon.

Brisket of beef

cooking time: 36 minutes
pressure: high

you will need for 6–8 servings:

METRIC/IMPERIAL

2 tablespoons oil	450 g/1 lb onions, sliced
1·5-kg/3-lb beef brisket, rolled and tied	600 ml/1 pint Guinness
4 rashers streaky bacon, rind removed	150 ml/¼ pint vinegar
	bay leaf
	bouquet garni

1 Put the joint and the oil in the cooker with the trivet removed. Brown joint on all sides and drain off excess fat.
2 Line the base of the cooker with the bacon, put the

meat on top, and pack onions all around it. Season and add spices. Pour in the liquids, making sure the cooker is no more than half full.

Bring to high pressure and cook for 36 minutes, or at the rate of 12 minutes per half kilo/per lb according to weight. Reduce pressure at room temperature. Either thicken the juices with flour blended with water, cook for a minute and serve separately, or use as a base for a soup. Serve brisket either hot or cold.

Variation:

If the meat is to be served hot, other vegetables could be added, provided the cooker is large enough. Cook for 27 minutes, reduce pressure with cold water, add prepared vegetables, bring to high pressure and cook for remaining 5 minutes.

Marinated collar of bacon

cooking time: 24 minutes
pressure: high

you will need for 6–8 servings:

METRIC/IMPERIAL

1 large onion, chopped	freshly ground pepper
2 teaspoons dried crushed rosemary	2 bay leaves
	sprig of parsley
2 teaspoons dried thyme	1-kg/2-lb Danish collar
300 ml/½ pint red wine	joint

Put the onion, herbs, wine, pepper, bay leaves and parsley in a saucepan. Heat gently, stir, then allow to cool.

Place the bacon in a bowl and cover it with the marinade. Leave it to stand for 24 hours, turning occasionally.

Put the bacon and marinade in the cooker with the trivet removed, making sure the cooker is no more than half full. Bring to high pressure and cook for 24 minutes or 12 minutes per half kilo/per lb according to weight.

Reduce pressure at room temperature and serve either hot or cold.

Cider and bacon braise

cooking time: 30 minutes
pressure: high

you will need for 6 servings:

METRIC/IMPERIAL

1-kg/2-lb piece smoked hock end of bacon	350 g/12 oz turnips, peeled and cut in quarters
450 ml/¾ pint dry cider	
2 bay leaves	2 leeks, washed, cut into 5-cm/2-inch lengths
sprig of parsley	
4 sticks celery, cut in thick slices	
350 g/12 oz even-sized carrots, peeled and whole	

1 With the trivet removed put the bacon in and half fill the cooker with cold water. Bring slowly to the boil in the open cooker, then throw the water away.
2 Put the joint back in the cooker, add the cider, bay leaves and parsley. Bring to high pressure and cook for 15 minutes per half kilo/per lb.
3 Ten minutes before the end of the cooking time reduce pressure with cold water. Add the vegetables and return to high pressure for a further 10 minutes.
4 Reduce pressure at room temperature, transfer the bacon to a heated serving dish, and surround it with the vegetables. Discard the bay leaves and parsley.
5 If liked, thicken the liquor with 1 tablespoon cornflour and cook for a minute. Serve separately.

Hint:

If using a gammon slipper or piece of collar, allow 12 minutes per half kilo/per lb.

Boiled beef in ale

cooking time: 30 minutes
pressure: high

you will need for 6 servings:

METRIC/IMPERIAL

1-kg/2-lb joint salted silverside	bouquet garni
	450 g/1 lb carrots, peeled
300 ml/½ pint pale ale	4 medium onions
150 ml/¼ pint water	

1 Place the joint in the cooker with the trivet removed. Add the ale, water and bouquet garni. Bring to high pressure and cook for 20 minutes.
2 Reduce pressure with cold water, add the carrots and onions. Return to high pressure and cook for 10 minutes. Reduce pressure with cold water.
3 Transfer the joint to a warmed serving dish and surround with the vegetables.
4 If liked, thicken the liquor with a little cornflour. Cook for a minute and serve separately.

Variations:

a Dumplings could be made with 100 g/4 oz self-raising flour, 50 g/2 oz prepared suet. Add the dumplings at the end of the cooking time and cook in the open cooker with a plate or the lid placed lightly on top for 10 minutes.
b Water can be used instead of the ale.
c Cider would add a nice flavour to the meat.
d Quartered cabbage could be added with the onions and carrots to serve as an extra vegetable.

Pot-au-feu

cooking time: 30 minutes
pressure: high

you will need for 4–6 servings:

METRIC/IMPERIAL

1-kg/2-lb piece boned shin of beef	2 large carrots, cut into thick pieces
bay leaf	1 large onion, cut into quarters
bouquet garni	
450 ml/¾ pint water	2 sticks celery, cut into large pieces
1½ beef stock cubes	
2 leeks, washed and cut into large pieces	salt and pepper

1 Tie the beef at intervals with string or tape.
2 Place the beef in the cooker with the trivet removed, cover with cold water, bring to the boil in the open cooker, then throw away the water.
3 Return the beef to the cooker with the bay leaf, bouquet garni, measured water and the crumbled stock cubes. Bring to high pressure and cook for 25 minutes. Reduce pressure with cold water.
4 Add the vegetables, salt and pepper, return to high pressure and cook for a further 5 minutes. Reduce pressure at room temperature.
5 Serve the meat in chunks with potatoes and the vegetables. The gravy can be served separately, thickened if preferred.

Variation:

Serve with horseradish sauce, or capers, chopped gherkins or mustard.

Casseroled leg of lamb

cooking time: 23 minutes or 10 minutes
                     per half kilo/per lb
pressure: high

you will need for 4–6 servings:

METRIC/IMPERIAL

½ leg of lamb (1 kg/2 lb)	100 g/4 oz button mushrooms, washed
25 g/1 oz dripping or lard	
300 ml/½ pint stock	25 g/1 oz plain flour
¼ teaspoon dried rosemary	salt and pepper
rind of 1 small lemon	
350 g/12 oz leeks, washed thoroughly	

1 Remove any excess fat from the lamb. Melt the dripping or lard in the cooker with the trivet removed, put in the lamb and brown it all over.
2 Add the stock, rosemary and lemon rind. Bring to high pressure and allow 10 minutes per half kilo/per lb. Reduce pressure at room temperature.
3 Cut the leeks into 2-cm/1-inch lengths, add to the cooker with the mushrooms. Return to high pressure and cook for 3 minutes. Reduce pressure at room temperature.
4 Transfer the lamb to a warmed serving dish. Using a slotted spoon, arrange the vegetables round the meat.

5 Blend the flour with a little water and stir into the meat juices. Bring to the boil, stirring, and cook for 1 minute. Season to taste.
6 Either pour the thickened gravy over the meat or serve separately.

Variations:

a Use carrots instead of mushrooms.
b Use half water or stock and half dry cider.
c Half water and half wine would also be a nice change.

Tongue with mustard sauce

cooking time: 37 minutes and 2 hours soaking time
pressure: high

you will need for 6 servings:

METRIC/IMPERIAL

1·25-kg/2½-lb ox tongue	20 g/¾ oz flour
2 carrots	300 ml/½ pint milk
3 sticks celery	150 ml/¼ pint cooking liquor from the tongue
3 cloves	
1 onion	2–3 teaspoons dry mustard
10–12 peppercorns	
few sprigs of parsley	2 teaspoons wine vinegar
bay leaf	pinch pepper

for sauce:
20 g/¾ oz butter

1 Place the tongue in a bowl, cover with cold water and leave it to soak for 2 hours.
2 Slice the carrots lengthways, coarsely chop the celery and stick the cloves into the peeled onion.
3 Transfer the tongue to the cooker with the trivet removed. Add the prepared vegetables, the peppercorns, parsley and bay leaf and enough water to half fill the pressure cooker. Bring to high pressure and cook for 37 minutes.
4 Allow the pressure to reduce at room temperature. Lift the tongue on to a board and when cool enough to handle, remove the skin, gristle and small bones.
5 Cut into slices and place on a serving dish. Spoon over 1 tablespoon of the cooking liquor, cover with foil and keep warm while making the sauce.
6 To make the sauce, melt the butter in a pan, add the flour and cook for 2 minutes, stirring. Gradually stir in the milk and cooking liquor. Bring to the boil and simmer for 2–3 minutes.
7 Blend the mustard powder with the vinegar and add to the sauce: add pepper to taste. Serve either poured over the tongue slices, or separately.

Variations:

a Serve with a Madeira sauce. Make an Espagnole sauce and add 3 tablespoons Madeira after straining. Reheat, and adjust seasoning.
b Serve with a Bigarade sauce. Make an Espagnole sauce, strain and add the juice of an orange or a lemon. A few shreds of the rind can be blanched and added to the sauce.
To make 300 ml/½ pint Espagnole sauce: Dice 1 carrot, 1 onion and 2 rashers of bacon. Melt 25 g/1 oz butter

in a heavy-based pan and fry the vegetables and bacon until golden. Blend in 25 g/1 oz flour, stirring the roux until brown. Gradually blend in 300 ml/ ½ pint well-flavoured brown stock, stirring constantly until the mixture thickens. Add a bouquet garni, cover the pan, set on an asbestos sheet and simmer for 30 minutes. Add 150 ml/¼ pint stock and blend in 2 tablespoons tomato purée. Cover and continue cooking for 30 minutes, stirring frequently. Strain before serving.

Gammon pot roast

cooking time: 36 minutes
pressure: high

you will need for 6–8 servings:

METRIC/IMPERIAL
1·5-kg/3-lb gammon joint   225 g/8 oz carrots, sliced
450 ml/¾ pint water   225 g/8 oz swede, diced
1 onion, peeled   toasted breadcrumbs
bay leaf

to garnish:
watercress

Place the gammon in the cooker with the trivet removed. Cover with water and bring slowly to the boil in the open cooker. Drain away the water.
Pour the measured 450 ml/¾ pint water into the cooker, add the onion and the bay leaf. Bring to high pressure and cook for 33 minutes. Reduce pressure with water.
Add the swede and carrot, return to high pressure and cook for 3 minutes. Reduce pressure with cold water.
Remove the joint, peel off the rind and press the toasted breadcrumbs on to the fat.
Place on a serving dish, and arrange the vegetables round the meat. To serve, garnish with the watercress.

Variation:
Instead of adding the carrot and swede and toasted breadcrumbs, remove the rind and coat the gammon in demerara sugar, stick the joint with cloves and place under a hot grill so as to just melt and brown the sugar.

Casseroles

The most popular use for the pressure cooker is with casseroles, for which it has endless scope. Instead of the long, slow cooking required for the tougher cuts of meat, a pressure cooker can produce well-cooked, tender meat in 25–30 minutes.
Depending on the quantities used, it is sometimes possible to cook the accompanying vegetables in the separators on the trivet above the casserole for the last 5 minutes of the cooking time.

● **Hints:**
a Sometimes the meat can be tossed in flour before being cooked, but as a general rule it is best to add the thickening in the open cooker at the end of cooking process.
b If using your own recipe the quantity of liquid may be varied. There should never be less than 300 ml/½ pint liquid, however, except in the case of quick-cooking meats which need only a short cooking time, as will be seen in some of the following recipes.

Beef hotpot

cooking time: 15 minutes
pressure: high

you will need for 4 servings:

METRIC/IMPERIAL
675 g/1½ lb shin of beef   1 (220-g/7¾-oz) can
1 tablespoon flour   curried beans with
4 sticks celery, sliced   sultanas
1 large onion, chopped   salt and pepper
450 ml/¾ pint beef stock
1 (220-g/7¾-oz) can baked
  beans

1 Cut the beef into 2·5-cm/1-inch cubes, toss in a little flour.
2 Place the meat in the cooker with the trivet removed, add the celery, onion and stock, making sure the cooker is no more than half full. Stir round.
3 Bring to high pressure and cook for 15 minutes. Reduce pressure at room temperature.
4 Stir in the remaining ingredients and heat through in the open cooker for a few minutes. Season to taste.

Harvest casserole

cooking time: 20 minutes
pressure: high

you will need for 4 servings:

METRIC/IMPERIAL
2 tablespoons oil   100 g/4 oz button
450 g/1 lb stewing beef,   mushrooms
  cut into 2-cm/1-inch   3 tomatoes, skinned and
  cubes   chopped
1 onion, sliced   1 (326-g/11½-oz) can
225 g/8 oz carrots   sweet corn
salt and pepper   bay leaf
300 ml/½ pint beef stock   1 tablespoon cornflour
25 g/1 oz short-cut
  macaroni

1 Heat the oil in the cooker with the trivet removed, add the meat and onions. Cook gently to brown them.
2 Stir in the carrots, salt, pepper and stock, bring to the boil, and stir in the macaroni. Add the mushrooms, tomatoes, sweet corn and bay leaf.
3 Bring to high pressure and cook for 20 minutes. Reduce heat at room temperature.
4 Blend the cornflour with a little water, add some hot stock and return to cooker.
5 Bring to the boil, stirring, and cook until thickened. Remove bay leaf and serve.

Variation:

If liked, open the cooker after 15 minutes and add 350 g/12 oz diced potato. Return to high pressure and cook for 5 minutes. There would be no need to thicken with the cornflour. Serve sprinkled with parsley.

Beef braise with port

cooking time: 10 minutes
pressure: high

you will need for 4 servings:

METRIC/IMPERIAL
575 g/1¼ lb (4 pieces)   salt and pepper
  chuck steak   1 medium onion, chopped
3 tablespoons port   100 g/4 oz streaky bacon,
2 tablespoons oil   cut into pieces
1 teaspoon dried oregano   150 ml/¼ pint stock
1 clove garlic, crushed

1 Trim the meat and place in a shallow dish. Pour over it the port, 1 tablespoon oil, the oregano, crushed garlic, salt and pepper. Leave on one side for at least 3 hours, turning frequently.
2 With the trivet removed, heat the remaining oil in the cooker, add the onion and bacon and cook for a few minutes.
3 Put in meat and marinade and add the remaining ingredients. Bring to high pressure and cook for 10 minutes.
4 Reduce pressure at room temperature.

Goulash with caraway

cooking time: 15 minutes
pressure: high

you will need for 4 servings:

METRIC/IMPERIAL
1 kg/2 lb stewing beef   150 ml/¼ pint beef stock
1 tablespoon oil   2 teaspoons paprika
225 g/8 oz onions, sliced   pepper
1 (227-g/8-oz) can peeled   salt
  tomatoes   pinch caraway seeds

1 Trim the beef into 2-cm/1-inch cubes.

2 Heat the oil in the cooker with the trivet removed, add the meat and stir round. Add the onions and cook for a few minutes to lightly brown.
3 Stir in the remaining ingredients. Bring to high pressure and cook for 15 minutes.
4 Reduce pressure at room temperature. Serve with noodles.

Quick stroganoff

cooking time: 15 minutes
pressure: high

you will need for 6 servings:

METRIC/IMPERIAL
2 tablespoons oil   175 g/6 oz button
1 kg/2 lb chuck steak,   mushrooms, washed and
  cut into strips   quartered
1 onion, sliced   freshly ground pepper
1 (298-g/10½-oz) can   2 tablespoons cornflour
  condensed mushroom   1 (142-ml/5-fl oz) carton
  soup   natural yogurt
½ can of water

1 Heat the oil in the cooker with the trivet removed, add the meat and fry quickly to brown all over.
2 Take out the meat, stir in the onions and fry fairly quickly to lightly brown.
3 Blend the condensed soup gradually with the water to break up lumps. Add to the cooker with the browned meat, mushrooms and pepper, making sure the cooker is no more than half full.
4 Bring to high pressure and cook for 15 minutes. Reduce pressure at room temperature.
5 Blend the cornflour with a little water and add some hot liquor to it: pour into the stew and cook for a minute in the open cooker to thicken.
6 Just before serving, stir in the yogurt and adjust seasoning. Serve with rice or noodles and a tossed salad.

Beef with horseradish

cooking time: 10 minutes
pressure: high

you will need for 2 servings:

METRIC/IMPERIAL
350-g/12-oz slice flank of   salt and pepper
  beef   1 tablespoon cornflour
1 medium onion, sliced   1 tablespoon horseradish
25 g/1 oz butter   sauce
300 ml/½ pint beef stock

1 Cut the beef into strips. With the trivet removed put the beef in the cooker with the onion, butter or margarine. Cook fairly quickly to seal the meat and lightly brown the onion.

Add the stock, salt and pepper, making sure the cooker is no more than half full. Bring to high pressure and cook for 10 minutes. Reduce pressure at room temperature.

Blend the cornflour with a little water, add some hot stock and return to the cooker with the horseradish. Bring just to the boil, stir and simmer until thickened, about 2 minutes.

Variation:
Use French mustard to taste, instead of horseradish. If using the mustard, half the stock could be red wine.

Beef stew with mustard dumplings

cooking time: 20 minutes
pressure: high

you will need for 4 servings:

METRIC/IMPERIAL

1 tablespoon cooking oil	40 g/1½ oz seasoned flour
1 large onion, chopped	225 g/8 oz carrots, sliced
2 sticks celery, chopped	600 ml/1 pint beef stock
675 g/1½ lb chuck or stewing steak, cut into 2-cm/1-inch cubes	2 tablespoons tomato purée

for dumplings:

100 g/4 oz self-raising flour	50 g/2 oz suet
1 teaspoon salt	3–4 tablespoons water
2 teaspoons mustard powder	

to garnish:
chopped parsley

Place the oil, onion and celery in the cooker with the trivet removed: cook gently for about 3 minutes. Toss the meat in the seasoned flour, add to the vegetables and fry to lightly brown.

Add the carrots, stock and tomato purée and stir round. Bring to high pressure and cook for 20 minutes. Reduce pressure at room temperature.

Meanwhile make the dumplings. Sieve the flour, salt and mustard together. Stir in the suet and water, mix to a soft dough with a knife and form into 8 small balls.

Remove the lid from the cooker and return it to the heat. Bring liquid to the boil and add the dumplings. Cover with a large plate and simmer for 10 minutes. Serve sprinkled with chopped parsley.

Variation:
Add some herbs to the suet pastry, with a little grated lemon rind instead of the mustard.

A few chopped walnuts added to the dumplings will give extra texture.

Beef stew with artichokes

cooking time: 15 minutes
pressure: high

you will need for 4 servings:

METRIC/IMPERIAL

675 g/1½ lb stewing steak, cubed	350 g/12 oz Jerusalem artichokes, peeled and sliced
150 ml/¼ pint red cooking wine	225 g/8 oz American long-grained rice
300 ml/½ pint beef stock	600 ml/1 pint water
2 teaspoons chopped tarragon	1 teaspoon salt
25 g/1 oz dripping	1 tablespoon cornflour
1 large onion, sliced	salt and pepper

1 Marinate the meat in red wine, stock and the chopped tarragon for as long as possible; overnight is best. Drain, but reserve the marinade for cooking.
2 Heat the dripping in the cooker with the trivet removed, add the meat and cook until well browned. Add onion and continue to fry for 2 minutes.
3 Put in the marinade and sliced artichokes, making sure the cooker is no more than half full. Bring to high pressure and cook for 15 minutes. Reduce pressure with cold water.
4 Put rice, water and salt into a saucepan, bring to the boil and stir once. Lower heat to simmer, cover and cook for 15 minutes, or until rice is tender and liquid absorbed.
5 Blend cornflour with a little water and add to the stew. Bring to the boil while stirring and cooking for 2–3 minutes in the open pan until thickened.
6 Check seasoning and serve over a bed of cooked rice.

Rich beef stew

cooking time: 15 minutes
pressure: high

you will need for 4 servings:

METRIC/IMPERIAL

675 g/1½ lb stewing steak	2 tablespoons tomato purée
1 tablespoon plain flour	generous pinch dried thyme
salt and pepper	bay leaf
100 g/4 oz streaky bacon, chopped	grated rind of orange
1 tablespoon oil or cooking fat	300 ml/½ pint red wine
2 onions, sliced	150 ml/¼ pint water or stock
2 carrots, sliced	
2 sticks celery, sliced	

1 Cut meat into fairly small cubes, toss in seasoned flour.
2 Place bacon in cooker with the trivet removed and heat gently till fat starts to run. Add oil, onion, carrots and celery and cook for 5 minutes.
3 Put in the meat and cook, stirring until sealed all over. Add tomato purée, thyme, bay leaf, orange rind, wine and water.

4 Bring to high pressure and cook for 15 minutes. Reduce pressure at room temperature. Remove bay leaf.

5 Serve with boiled potatoes.

Spiced beef

cooking time: 2 hours 20 minutes
pressure: high

you will need for 6–8 servings:

METRIC/IMPERIAL

I kg/2 lb chuck steak	I green pepper, deseeded
2 teaspoons made mustard	and sliced
I clove garlic, crushed	I tablespoon oil
I tablespoon wine vinegar	225 g/8 oz salt pork or
coarsely grated rind and	streaky bacon, cut into
juice of I orange	pieces
salt and pepper	bay leaf
2 teaspoons	300 ml/½ pint beef stock
Worcestershire sauce	2 tablespoons plain flour
½ teaspoon ground ginger	
225 g/8 oz button onions,	
peeled and whole	

1 Trim the meat and cut into good-sized cubes.

2 Mix the mustard, garlic, vinegar, orange juice, salt and pepper, Worcestershire sauce and ginger together in a bowl.

3 Put in the meat, stir round and add the onions and green pepper. Cover and leave to stand for at least 2 hours.

4 Heat the oil in the cooker with the trivet removed and fry the salt pork until crisp. Add all the ingredients in the bowl, the bay leaf and stock.

5 Bring to high pressure and cook for 20 minutes Reduce pressure at room temperature.

6 Remove bay leaf. Blend the flour with a little water and hot liquor. Stir into the stew and bring it to the boil in the open cooker. Cook for one minute to thicken.

7 Bring the orange rind to the boil in a small pan of water, drain and sprinkle over the beef.

8 Serve with rice and a tossed salad.

Summer stew

cooking time: 20 minutes
pressure: high

you will need for 5–6 servings:

METRIC/IMPERIAL

I kg/2 lb chuck steak	bay leaf
50 g/2 oz dripping or lard	salt and pepper
2 onions, sliced	100 g/4 oz button
2 carrots, sliced	mushrooms
300 ml/½ pint beef stock	3 tablespoons plain flour
I (397-g/14-oz) can peeled	225 g/8 oz courgettes,
tomatoes	sliced

1 Trim the meat and cut into 3-cm/1½-inch cubes.

2 Heat the fat in the cooker with the trivet removed and fry the meat quickly to brown all over. Transfer it with a slotted spoon on to a plate.

3 Fry the onion until golden, about 5 minutes. Stir in the carrots and cook for 2 minutes.

4 Return the meat to the pan with the stock, tomatoes bay leaf, salt and pepper, making sure that the cooker is no more than half full. Bring to high pressure and cook for 20 minutes. Reduce pressure at room temperature.

5 Blend the flour with a little water to remove lumps. Add some of the hot liquor, stir into the stew and bring it to the boil in the open cooker. Reduce the heat and cook for 2 minutes.

6 Stir in the mushrooms and courgettes: bring to high pressure and cook for 3 minutes. Reduce pressure at room temperature.

Beef stew with beer

cooking time: 20 minutes
pressure: high

you will need for 6 servings:

METRIC/IMPERIAL

I kg/2 lb chuck steak	I (64-g/2¼-oz) can tomato
50 g/2 oz plain flour	purée
salt and pepper	I (250-ml/9¼-fl oz) can
40 g/1½ oz butter or	Guinness
margarine	150 ml/¼ pint water
I tablespoon corn oil	I teaspoon vinegar
2 onions, quartered	2 bay leaves
I clove garlic	
100 g/4 oz button	
mushrooms, washed	

1 Trim the meat and cut into cubes. Toss them in seasoned flour and reserve the rest of the flour.

2 Melt the butter or margarine with the oil in the cooker with the trivet removed, and fry the meat until brown on all sides, stirring frequently.

3 Add the onions, garlic and mushrooms, stir round and cook for 2–3 minutes.

4 Stir in the tomato purée, Guinness, water, vinegar and bay leaves, making sure the cooker is no more than half full. Bring to high pressure and cook for minutes. Reduce pressure at room temperature.

5 Blend the remaining flour with a little water, add some of the hot liquid: return mixture to the cooker stir round, and bring to the boil, stirring. Cook for minute to thicken.

Variation:

Instead of the mushrooms, add 100 g/4 oz dried prunes.

● **Hint:**

Prunes will need to be covered with boiling water for 15 minutes before using. Drain and add with an extra 150 ml/¼ pint water.

Beef olives with horseradish

cooking time: 15 minutes
pressure: high

you will need for 4 servings:

METRIC/IMPERIAL
8 very thin slices rump
  steak, about 575 g/1¼ lb
1 tablespoon oil

for stuffing:
1 tablespoon oil
1 onion, finely chopped
75 g/3 oz fresh white
  breadcrumbs
1 tablespoon chopped
  parsley
grated rind of ½ lemon
  (optional)

100 g/4 oz mushrooms,
  sliced
300 ml/½ pint beef stock

2 teaspoons horseradish
  sauce
salt and pepper
1 medium egg, well
  beaten
1 tablespoon milk

To make the stuffing, put the oil in a saucepan, add the onion and cook until soft without browning. Remove pan from the heat and stir in the remaining stuffing ingredients so that the mixture binds together.

Lay the pieces of meat on a board and beat them out flat with a rolling pin.

Divide the stuffing between each piece, placing it in the centre. Roll up and tie them with a thin piece of string or cotton.

Heat 1 tablespoon oil in the cooker with the trivet removed and fry the beef olives quickly to brown them all over.

Add the mushrooms and stock, making sure the cooker is no more than half full, then bring to high pressure and cook for 15 minutes. Reduce pressure at room temperature.

Remove the beef olives with a slotted spoon, and taking off the string or cotton, place them on a heated serving dish to keep hot.

If liked, thicken the sauce by blending 25 g/1 oz plain flour with a little water, add a little hot liquid, return to the pan, bring to the boil, stirring, and cook for 2 minutes. Spoon over the beef.

Variation:
Use veal instead of beef: use chicken stock and some herbs for the stuffing.

Chilli con carne

cooking time: 15 minutes
pressure: high

you will need for 4 servings:

METRIC/IMPERIAL
175 g/6 oz red kidney
  beans
2 tablespoons pure corn
  oil
450 g/1 lb mince

1 onion, sliced
1–2 teaspoons chilli powder
1 (43-g/1½-oz) packet
  tomato soup
600 ml/1 pint water

1 Put beans in a bowl, cover them with boiling water, cover the bowl and leave to stand for 1 hour.
2 Heat the oil in the cooker with the trivet removed, add the beef with the onion and chilli powder and sauté until lightly browned.
3 Stir in the tomato soup mix and water and bring to the boil, stirring all the time.
4 Add the kidney beans and, making sure the cooker is no more than half full, bring to high pressure and cook for 15 minutes.
5 Reduce pressure at room temperature and serve with plainly boiled rice or mashed potatoes.

Chilli bean and beef stew

cooking time: 20 minutes
pressure: high

you will need for 4 servings:

METRIC/IMPERIAL
575 g/1¼ lb chuck steak
2 tablespoons oil
1 onion, chopped
300 ml/½ pint beef stock
1 tablespoon tomato purée
salt and pepper
½–2 teaspoons chilli
  powder, depending on
  strength

2 tablespoons plain flour
2 canned red peppers, cut
  into strips
1 (432-g/15¼-oz) can red
  kidney beans

1 Trim the beef into large, neat cubes.
2 Heat the oil in the cooker with the trivet removed, add the onion and cook for 5 minutes.
3 Put the meat in, stir round and cook to brown it all over.
4 Stir in the stock, purée, salt, pepper and chilli powder to taste, making sure that the cooker is no more than half full. Bring to high pressure and cook for 20 minutes. Reduce pressure at room temperature.
5 Blend the flour with a little water to remove any lumps, stir in some of the hot liquid and add it to the pan. Bring to the boil, stirring and simmer for 2 minutes.
6 Add the peppers and the kidney beans, well drained. Heat through for a few minutes.

Braised beef with tomato and wine sauce

cooking time: 15 minutes
pressure: high

you will need for 4 servings:

METRIC/IMPERIAL
1 tablespoon corn oil
575 g/1¼ lb chuck steak,
  cut into 4 pieces
1 onion, sliced
225 g/8 oz tomatoes,
  peeled

to garnish:
chopped parsley

5 tablespoons red wine
200 ml/7 fl oz meat stock
½ teaspoon dried oregano
pepper
2 tablespoons plain flour

1 Heat the corn oil in the cooker with the trivet removed. Put in the meat and lightly brown it on both sides. Take out the meat and keep it on one side.
2 Place the onion in the oil and cook to brown lightly: add the tomatoes, wine, meat stock, herbs and pepper, making sure that the cooker is no more than half full.
3 Replace the meat, bring to high pressure and cook for 15 minutes. Reduce pressure under cold running water. Transfer the meat to a heated serving dish, and keep hot.
4 Blend the flour with a little water making sure there are no lumps. Add a little of the hot liquid to the blended flour and pour into the cooker.
5 Bring to the boil, stirring, until the sauce thickens: reduce heat and cook for 2 minutes.
6 Pour over the steak and sprinkle with chopped parsley.

Variation:
Use 150 ml/¼ pint light ale instead of the wine and make up to 300 ml/½ pint with stock. Add a stick of celery, sliced.

Boeuf bourguignon

cooking time: 20 minutes
pressure: high

you will need for 6 servings:

METRIC/IMPERIAL
I kg/2 lb chuck steak	I clove garlic, crushed
25 g/I oz flour	4 tablespoons brandy
salt and pepper	100 g/4 oz mushrooms,
50 g/2 oz unsalted butter	washed
I tablespoon corn oil	I tablespoon tomato purée
100 g/4 oz button onions,	450 ml/¾ pint red wine
peeled	15 g/½ oz flour
100 g/4 oz bacon, rind	
removed	

to garnish:
chopped parsley

1 Cut the meat into cubes. Season the flour with salt and pepper and roll the meat in the flour.
2 Melt 40 g/1½ oz of the butter and the oil in the cooker with the trivet removed and brown the meat gradually, removing it when ready with a slotted spoon.
3 Brown the onions in the cooker. Cut the bacon in pieces and add it with the garlic.
4 Return the meat to the cooker, heat a little then pour in the brandy and ignite carefully.
5 Stir in the mushrooms, tomato purée and wine making sure the cooker is no more than half full Bring to high pressure and cook for 20 minutes Reduce pressure at room temperature.
6 Blend the remaining butter and flour together to make a beurre manié and add in pieces to the beef. Stir round until dissolved, bring to the boil and simmer for 2 minutes to cook the thickening.
7 Serve sprinkled with chopped parsley.

Savoury steak

cooking time: 15 minutes
pressure: high

you will need for 4 servings:

METRIC/IMPERIAL
450 g/I lb stewing steak	I (43-g/1½-oz) packet
100 g/4 oz ox kidney	Oxtail soup
2 tablespoons pure corn	600 ml/I pint water
oil	100 g/4 oz button
I onion, sliced	mushrooms

1 Trim the steak and kidney and cut into cubes.
2 Heat the oil in the cooker with the trivet removed add the meat and onion and sauté until lightly browned. Add the oxtail soup mix and water and bring to the boil, stirring all the time.
3 Making sure the cooker is no more than half full add the mushrooms, bring to high pressure and cool for 15 minutes. Reduce pressure at room temperature.
4 Serve with mashed potato.

Variation:
Use either tomato or mushroom soup mix.

Winter lamb hotpot

cooking time: 15 minutes
pressure: high

you will need for 4 servings:

METRIC/IMPERIAL
2 medium onions, sliced	I kg/2 lb middle neck of
thickly	lamb, in pieces
225 g/8 oz carrots, sliced	salt and pepper
thickly	sprig of rosemary
I (43-g/1½-oz) packet	450 g/I lb potatoes,
Swiss garden vegetable	peeled and sliced
soup	

to garnish:
chopped parsley

1 Put the onions in the cooker with the trivet removed add the carrots and sprinkle in the soup mix.
2 Stir in 600 ml/1 pint water, place the pieces of lamb on top of the vegetables, making sure the cooker i no more than half full. Season and add rosemary.
3 Bring to high pressure and cook for 10 minutes Reduce pressure with cold water.
4 Arrange the potatoes over the top, return to high pressure and cook for 5 minutes.
5 Serve sprinkled with chopped parsley.

Variations:
a Use other varieties of soup, such as tomato or leek
b Cook the potatoes separately. Arrange the meat in casserole, place the sliced potatoes on top, brush with butter and place under a moderate grill until th potatoes are lightly browned.

Lamb and vegetable casserole

cooking time: 10 minutes and 5 minutes
pressure: high

you will need for 6 servings:

METRIC/IMPERIAL

1 kg/2 lb lamb chops	2 large onions, sliced
salt and pepper	225 g/8 oz carrots,
garlic powder	chopped
2 tablespoons flour	3 sticks celery, sliced
2 tablespoons vegetable	2 leeks, cleaned and sliced
oil	350 g/12 oz American
300 ml/½ pint meat stock	long-grain rice
1 bay leaf	600 ml/1 pint water
1 teaspoon dried thyme	

Season meat with salt, pepper and garlic powder.
Roll in flour. Heat the oil in the cooker with the
trivet removed and fry the meat on both sides until
browned.
Add stock and herbs. Bring to high pressure and
cook for 10 minutes. Reduce pressure immediately
with cold water.
Add onion, carrot, celery, leek, rice and water, bring
to the boil and stir once. Return to high pressure and
cook for a further 5 minutes.
Reduce pressure with cold water, remove bay leaf,
check seasoning and serve.

Lamb curry

cooking time: 15 minutes
pressure: high

you will need for 4 servings:

METRIC/IMPERIAL

450 g/1 lb lean top leg of	1 clove garlic, crushed
lamb	pinch sugar
2 tablespoons oil	¼ teaspoon salt
1 large onion, chopped	300 ml/½ pint chicken
2 tablespoons curry	stock
powder	225 g/8 oz long-grain rice
1 eating apple, chopped	400 ml/scant ¾ pint water
1 banana, sliced	salt and pepper
1 tablespoon mango	1 teaspoon turmeric
chutney, chopped	(optional)
1 tablespoon tomato purée	

Remove excess fat from the lamb and dice the meat.
Heat the oil in the cooker with the trivet removed,
put in the meat and cook for a few minutes. Add the
onion and curry powder, stir round and continue to
cook for a short time.
Add the remaining ingredients, except the rice, in the
order listed, making sure the cooker is no more than
half full. Bring to high pressure and cook for 10
minutes. Reduce pressure with cold water.
Put the rice into an ovenproof dish which will fit into
the cooker, add salt, pepper and turmeric, if liked.
Pour in the boiling water, stir and cover with a piece
of foil, turning the edge under the rim of the dish.

5 Place the trivet in the cooker over the meat and
stand the dish of rice on top. Bring to high pressure
and cook for 5 minutes. Reduce pressure at room
temperature.
6 Serve with dessicated coconut, redcurrant jelly and
salted peanuts.

Lamb and mung bean stew

cooking time: 20 minutes
pressure: high

you will need for 4 servings:

METRIC/IMPERIAL

1 lean breast of lamb,	1 (396-g/14-oz) can
boned	tomatoes
2 tablespoons oil	salt and pepper
2 medium onions, chopped	300 ml/½ pint stock (or
225 g/8 oz dried mung	water and stock cube)
beans	

1 Using a sharp knife, cut off as much meat from the
lamb as possible.
2 Place the lamb, oil and onions in the cooker with the
trivet removed, stir round and cook for a few minutes.
3 Wash the beans, drain and add with the remaining
ingredients.
4 Bring to high pressure and cook for 20 minutes.
Reduce pressure with cold water.
5 Serve with chunks of bread.

Basic lamb stew

cooking time: 20 minutes
pressure: high

you will need for 8 servings:

METRIC/IMPERIAL

1·5 kg/3 lb boned	2 teaspoons vegetable
shoulder of lamb	extract
3 tablespoons oil	2 teaspoons tomato purée
2 large onions, chopped	freshly ground pepper
3 carrots	3 tablespoons cornflour
600 ml/1 pint meat stock	

1 Trim the meat and cut into 2·5-cm/1-inch cubes.
2 Heat the oil in the cooker with the trivet removed,
add the onion and cook until lightly browned. Stir in
the carrots and cook for 1 minute. Remove the
vegetables with a slotted spoon.
3 Put in the meat, stir round to lightly brown, return
the onion and carrots and add stock, vegetable
extract, tomato purée, salt and pepper, making sure
the cooker is no more than half full.
4 Bring to high pressure and cook for 20 minutes.
Reduce pressure at room temperature.
5 Blend the cornflour with a little water to remove any
lumps, stir in a little hot stock, then add to cooker.
Bring to the boil, stirring, reduce heat and simmer
until thickened, about 3 minutes.

6 Serve one third immediately, if required, and freeze the remainder in two lots.

to freeze:
Allow to become cold and freeze two lots in plastic containers, a polythene freezer bag or a foil parcel placed in the cooker separators.

to thaw:
Slightly thaw the parcel and remove freezer bag, wrap stew in foil, replace it in the separator, and put 300 ml/½ pint water in the cooker. Put the separator on the trivet, bring to high pressure and cook for 8 minutes.

Variations:
a After thawing, add 225 g/8 oz cooked mixed vegetables, put in a pie dish and cover with a pastry lid. Bake in the oven as for any pastry pie.
b Add a little wine or sherry to the thawed portion of stew, 100 g/4 oz mushrooms and a little soured cream or yogurt.
c As an alternative, add 1 tablespoon demerara sugar, 2 teaspoons soy sauce, 1 small green pepper and the drained contents of a small can pineapple pieces.

Lamb, turnip and pea stew with rice

cooking time: 15 minutes
pressure: high

you will need for 4 servings:

METRIC/IMPERIAL

75 g/3 oz split peas	1 teaspoon rosemary
50 g/2 oz dripping	225 g/8 oz American
675 g/1½ lb stewing lamb	long-grain rice
pieces	600 ml/1 pint water
1 large onion, chopped	1 teaspoon salt
225 g/8 oz turnip,	1 tablespoon cornflour
chopped	salt and pepper
600 ml/1 pint meat stock	

1 Soak split peas in hot water for 1 hour.
2 Heat the dripping in the cooker with the trivet removed, fry the meat until browned on all sides. Add onion and continue to cook for 2 minutes.
3 Add turnip, soaked peas, stock and rosemary, making sure the cooker is no more than half full. Bring to high pressure and cook for 15 minutes. Reduce pressure with cold water.
4 Put rice, water and salt into a saucepan. Bring to the boil and stir once. Lower heat to simmer, cover and cook for 15 minutes, or until rice is tender and liquid absorbed.
5 Add a little water to the cornflour and mix into the lamb stew. Bring to the boil, stirring, and cook for 2–3 minutes in the open pan until thickened.
6 Check seasoning and serve over a bed of rice.

Herbed lamb

cooking time: 20 minutes and 15 minutes
pressure: high

you will need for 4–6 servings:

METRIC/IMPERIAL

½ leg of lamb, boned	300 ml/½ pint meat stock,
(keep the bones)	made from the bones
1 onion	2 tablespoons plain flour
for the marinade:	
4 tablespoons corn oil	1 teaspoon crushed
1 tablespoon lemon juice	rosemary
1 tablespoon tomato	½ teaspoon ground ginger
purée	salt and freshly ground
2 teaspoons	pepper
Worcestershire sauce	

1 Trim the fat and cut meat into 2-cm/1-inch cubes.
2 Make up the marinade, mix well together, add the meat and onion. Turn in the mixture and leave for about 2 hours.
3 Meanwhile, to make the stock, pour 300 ml/½ pint water into the cooker with the trivet removed and add the bones, making sure the cooker is no more than half full. Bring to high pressure and cook for 2 minutes.
4 Reduce pressure at room temperature. Strain the stock and make up to 300 ml/½ pint, if necessary.
5 Place the meat and marinade in the cooker with the trivet removed and fry fairly fast to seal in the meat juices.
6 Add the stock and stir round. Bring to high pressure and cook for 15 minutes. Reduce pressure at room temperature.
7 Blend the flour with a little water, add some of the hot liquor and return it to the cooker. Bring to simmering point, stirring, and cook for a few minutes to thicken.

Lamb chops with paprika

cooking time: 12 minutes
pressure: high

you will need for 4 servings:

METRIC/IMPERIAL

1 onion, sliced	salt and pepper
2 tablespoons paprika	450 g/1 lb potatoes,
1 (396-g/14-oz) can	peeled and quartered
tomatoes	150 ml/¼ pint soured
150 ml/¼ pint chicken	cream
stock	
675 g/1½ lb best end	
neck of lamb chops	

1 Place sliced onion and paprika in the cooker with the trivet removed and mix in the can of tomatoes and chicken stock. Bring to the boil, stirring to break up the tomatoes.
2 Season the lamb chops and arrange on top of the

sauce. Add potatoes and sprinkle with a little more seasoning.
Bring to high pressure and cook for 12 minutes. Reduce pressure at room temperature and transfer to serving dish. Pour cream over the top. Serve at once.

Lamb and butter beans

cooking time: 15–20 minutes
pressure: high

you will need for 4 servings:

METRIC/IMPERIAL
1 tablespoon oil	salt and pepper
1 large onion, sliced	1 (396-g/14-oz) can peeled
8 middle neck lamb chops	tomatoes
1 (425-g/15-oz) can butter	150 ml/¼ pint stock
beans	
¼ teaspoon dried crushed	
rosemary	

Heat the oil in the cooker with the trivet removed, put in the onion and cook for a few minutes. Add the middle neck lamb chops and the remaining ingredients. Bring to high pressure and cook for 15–20 minutes, depending on the thickness of the meat. Reduce pressure at room temperature. Serve with cabbage or Brussels sprouts.

Lamb chop casserole

cooking time: 10 minutes
pressure: high

you will need for 4 servings:

METRIC/IMPERIAL
1 kg/2 lb potatoes, peeled	salt and pepper
and sliced evenly	4 loin of lamb chops
1 large onion, sliced	2 teaspoons beef stock
175 g/6 oz mushrooms,	powder
washed and sliced	300 ml/½ pint boiling
225 g/8 oz tomatoes,	water
peeled and sliced	

Arrange half the potatoes in the cooker with the trivet removed, half the onion, mushrooms and tomatoes on top. Season with salt and pepper. Put the chops in a single layer on top of the vegetables. Sprinkle the stock powder over them and pour over the water.
Cover with the remaining onion, mushrooms and tomatoes: finish with a layer of potato, making sure the cooker is no more than half full. Season with a little salt and pepper.
Bring to high pressure and cook for 10 minutes. Reduce pressure at room temperature.

Variation:
Sprinkle the meat with a little dried marjoram or crushed rosemary, or put two sprigs of rosemary on the potato to give extra flavour.

● **Hint:**
It is important that the potatoes are even in thickness, say about 1-cm/½-inch pieces, otherwise some will be overcooked.

Swiss lamb with potato dumplings

cooking time: 15 minutes
pressure: high

you will need for 4 servings:

METRIC/IMPERIAL
575 g/1¼ lb stewing lamb	1 (43-g/1½-oz) packet
2 tablespoons pure corn	Swiss Garden vegetable
oil	soup
	600 ml/1 pint water

for dumplings:
450 g/1 lb cooked potato,	chopped parsley
mashed	little onion powder
1 egg yolk	
100 g/4 oz self-raising	
flour	

1 Trim the lamb and cut into cubes. Heat the oil in the cooker with the trivet removed and sauté the lamb until browned. Add the soup mix and water and bring to the boil, stirring.
2 Make sure the cooker is no more than half full, then bring to high pressure and cook for 15 minutes.
3 Blend together all the ingredients for the potato dumplings. Divide into 8 and form into balls.
4 Reduce pressure at room temperature, open the cooker and add the dumplings to the liquid. Return to high pressure and cook for a further 5 minutes.
5 Reduce pressure at room temperature and serve with cabbage.

Normandy pork

cooking time: 12 minutes
pressure: high

you will need for 4 servings:

METRIC/IMPERIAL
675 g/1½ lb lean pork	bay leaf
spare rib chops	grated rind and juice of ½
25 g/1 oz butter or lard	lemon
1 onion, chopped	300 ml/½ pint cider
salt and pepper	1 tablespoon cornflour
1 large eating apple, diced	

1 Remove the meat from the bones and discard excess fat: cut meat into cubes.
2 Heat the butter or lard in the cooker with the trivet removed, add the meat and onion and cook until lightly browned. Add seasoning, the apple, bay leaf, lemon rind and juice and the cider.

3 Bring to high pressure and cook for 12 minutes. Reduce pressure at room temperature and remove the bay leaf.

4 Blend the cornflour with a little water, stir in some hot stock and pour back into the cooker. Bring to the boil, stirring, and cook for 1 minute until thickened.

Variation:
Add raisins with the apple.

Pork and rice with corn

cooking time: 5 minutes
pressure: high

you will need for 4 servings:

METRIC/IMPERIAL

450 g/1 lb pork loin, cut in thin strips	1 teaspoon salt
2 tablespoons corn oil	$\frac{1}{2}$ teaspoon cumin
1 medium onion, chopped	$\frac{1}{2}$ teaspoon oregano
1 clove garlic, crushed	4 tablespoons apple purée
1 (326-g/11$\frac{1}{2}$-oz) can sweet corn kernels	600 ml/1 pint meat stock
	225 g/8 oz American long-grain rice

1 Place the oil in the cooker with the trivet removed, add the pork strips and cook all over to seal in the juices. Add the onion and garlic and fry gently.

2 Stir in the corn, seasonings, apple purée and stock. Bring to the boil in the open cooker: add the rice and stir once, making sure the cooker is no more than half full.

3 Bring to high pressure and cook for 5 minutes. Reduce pressure with cold water. Serve the rice with broccoli and tomatoes.

Spiced pork casserole

cooking time: 6 minutes
pressure: high

you will need for 4 servings:

METRIC/IMPERIAL

2 tablespoons oil	1 teaspoon French mustard
575 g/1$\frac{1}{4}$ lb pork fillet, cut into cubes	$\frac{1}{4}$ teaspoon ground ginger
1 large onion, chopped	$\frac{1}{4}$ teaspoon ground nutmeg
1 (213-g/7$\frac{1}{2}$-oz) can peach slices	1 teaspoon Worcestershire sauce
little chicken stock	salt and pepper
1 small green pepper, cut in strips and blanched	

1 Heat the oil in the cooker with the trivet removed, put in the pork and onion and cook quickly for 2 minutes to seal in the juices.

2 Strain the juice from the peaches and make it up to 150 ml/$\frac{1}{4}$ pint with stock. Keeping the peaches aside, add the juice and stock to the cooker. Bring to high pressure and cook for 6 minutes.

4 Reduce pressure with cold water. Put in the pepper and simmer gently in the open cooker.

5 Blend the mustard and spices together and add to the cooker. Stir round and cook for a few minutes to allow the flavour to develop in the meat. Add the peach slices to warm just before serving.

6 Serve with plain boiled rice and a tossed salad.

Pork and bean casserole

cooking time: 15 minutes
pressure: high

you will need for 4 servings:

METRIC/IMPERIAL

100 g/4 oz dried haricot beans	1 tablespoon cornflour
1 kg/2 lb pork belly	2 tablespoons water
15 g/$\frac{1}{2}$ oz dripping	1 tablespoon tomato purée
1 large onion, chopped	225 g/8 oz American long-grain rice
225 g/8 oz white cabbage, shredded	600 ml/1 pint water
300 ml/$\frac{1}{2}$ pint meat stock	1 teaspoon salt
salt and pepper	

1 Soak the beans in boiling water for 1 hour.

2 Remove any bones and excess fat from the pork and cube the meat.

3 Melt the dripping in the cooker with the trivet removed and cook the meat until it no longer looks pink.
Add onion and cabbage and fry for 3 minutes.

4 Add the drained beans, stock and seasoning to taste, making sure the cooker is no more than half full. Bring to high pressure and cook for 15 minutes, then, reduce pressure with cold water.

5 Meanwhile, put rice, water and salt into a saucepan. Bring to the boil and stir once. Lower heat to simmer, cover and cook for 15 minutes, or until the rice is tender and liquid absorbed.

6 Mix together the cornflour, water and tomato purée and add it to the pork mixture. Bring to the boil while stirring and cook for 2–3 minutes in the open pan until thickened.

7 Serve the pork and vegetables over the boiled rice.

Belly of pork casserole

cooking time: 15 minutes
pressure: high

you will need for 4 servings:

METRIC/IMPERIAL

575 g/1$\frac{1}{4}$ lb lean belly of pork	$\frac{1}{2}$ teaspoon made mustard
1 large onion, chopped	$\frac{1}{2}$ teaspoon dried sage (optional)
175 g/6 oz carrots, sliced	salt and pepper
300 ml/$\frac{1}{2}$ pint chicken stock	40 g/1$\frac{1}{2}$ oz sultanas
3 tablespoons tomato ketchup	15 g/$\frac{1}{2}$ oz plain flour

Remove rind and any bone from the pork and cut into cubes.

Place these in the cooker with the trivet removed and fry gently until the fat begins to run, then more quickly to brown the meat. Remove with a slotted spoon on to a plate.

Put in the onion and cook for 5 minutes to lightly brown: add the carrots and cook for 2 minutes. Return the meat to the pan with the stock, tomato ketchup, mustard, sage if used, salt and pepper, making sure that the cooker is no more than half full.

Cover and bring to high pressure and cook for 15 minutes. Reduce pressure at room temperature. Stir in the sultanas.

Blend the flour with 2 tablespoons water, making sure there are no lumps. Add some of the hot liquid, stir into the casserole, bring to the boil, stirring: reduce heat and cook for 2 minutes to thicken.

Parslied pork stew

cooking time: 25 minutes
pressure: high

you will need for 4–6 servings:

METRIC/IMPERIAL

450 g/I lb boned spare ribs of pork	300 ml/½ pint chicken or herb stock
I tablespoon corn oil	pepper
175 g/6 oz onion	350 g/12 oz small new potatoes of even size
100-g/4-oz smoked piece of gammon or forehock steak	

to garnish:
2 tablespoons chopped parsley

Cut the pork into 2-cm/1-inch cubes.
Heat the oil in the cooker with the trivet removed, add some of the meat and fry quickly to brown all over: transfer with a slotted spoon on to a plate. Fry the rest of the pork and transfer it to the plate.
Put in the onion and cook gently. Remove the rind from the gammon and cut the meat into strips. Add it to the onion, stir round and cook for a few minutes.
Return the pork to the cooker with the stock and pepper. Bring to high pressure and cook for 20 minutes.
Reduce pressure at room temperature. Add the potatoes, return to high pressure and cook for 5 minutes.
Reduce pressure at room temperature. Serve sprinkled with the chopped parsley.

Variations:
Use freshly chopped sage and grated lemon rind in the stew.
If liked, crushed garlic would give an interesting flavour to the dish.

c Instead of stock, try using tomato juice and mixed herbs.

d Chopped chives sprinkled over would make a change from a parsley garnish.

● **Hint:**
If new potatoes are not available, choose waxy old potatoes and cut into even-sized pieces.

Pork with red cabbage

cooking time: 12 minutes
pressure: high

you will need for 4 servings:

METRIC/IMPERIAL

I tablespoon corn oil	150 ml/¼ pint white wine vinegar
4 pork shoulder steaks	
25 g/I oz butter	150 ml/¼ pint water
50 g/2 oz demerara sugar	salt and pepper
25 g/I oz sultanas	
675 g/I½ lb red cabbage, shredded	

1 Heat the oil in the cooker with the trivet removed, add the pork steaks and fry to lightly brown each side. Transfer them to a plate.
2 Put in the rest of the ingredients and stir round.
3 Place the chops on the cabbage and, making sure the cooker is no more than half full, bring to high pressure and cook for 12 minutes.
4 Reduce pressure with cold water. Serve at once with mashed potato.

Variations:
a Using cider instead of water and vinegar, thicken the liquor with 1 tablespoon flour blended with a little water, and serve over the chops as a gravy.
b Add 1 onion and apple, sliced, and use 300 ml/½ pint cider for the cooking liquid.

Golden vegetable pork

cooking time: 25 minutes
pressure: high

you will need for 4 servings:

METRIC/IMPERIAL

450-g/I-lb piece of pork leg	600 ml/I pint water
2 tablespoons pure corn oil	I small green pepper, seeded and sliced
I (43-g/I½-oz) packet golden vegetable soup	100 g/4 oz button mushrooms, washed

1 Trim the pork and cut into cubes. Heat the oil in the cooker with the trivet removed, add the pork and sauté until lightly browned.
2 Mix in the golden vegetable soup and water and bring to the boil, stirring all the time. Add the green pepper and mushrooms.

3 Making sure the cooker is no more than half full bring to high pressure and cook for 25 minutes.

4 Reduce pressure at room temperature, serve with noodles.

Curried veal with apricots

cooking time: 12 minutes
pressure: high

you will need for 4 servings:

METRIC/IMPERIAL

100 g/4 oz dried apricots	300 ml/½ pint chicken
1 large onion, chopped	stock
25 g/1 oz butter or	salt and pepper
margarine	½ small green pepper,
1 tablespoon oil	blanched
1 tablespoon curry powder	1 tablespoon cornflour
575 g/1¼ lb stewing veal,	
cut into cubes	

1 Cover the apricots with boiling water and leave for 15 minutes.

2 Put the onion in the cooker, with the trivet removed, with the butter or margarine and oil. Cook gently for a few minutes, stir in the curry powder and cook for 1 minute. Stir in the veal and cook for 1 minute.

3 Add the stock, drained apricots, salt and pepper, making sure the cooker is no more than half full. Bring to high pressure and cook for 12 minutes.

4 Reduce pressure at room temperature. Add the pepper and cook in the open cooker for a few minutes.

5 Blend the cornflour with a little water, add some of the hot liquor to it and return it to the pan. Cook for 1 minute for the cornflour to thicken.

6 Serve with rice and usual accompaniments for curry; redcurrant jelly, salted peanuts, soured cream, tomato slices and chopped onion.

Ragoût of veal

cooking time: 15 minutes
pressure: high

you will need for 4 servings:

METRIC/IMPERIAL

175 ml/3 oz dried green	¼ teaspoon dried thyme
peas	¼ teaspoon ground mace
675 g/1½ lb boneless neck	or nutmeg
of veal	225 g/8 oz American
2 tablespoons flour	long-grain rice
40 g/1½ oz dripping	600 ml/1 pint water
8 small onions or shallots	1 teaspoon salt
3 carrots, sliced	1 tablespoon cornflour
600 ml/1 pint meat stock	salt and pepper

1 Pour boiling water on to the peas and soak them for 2 hours.

2 Cut the veal into serving pieces and dust with flour.

Melt dripping in the cooker with the trivet removed and fry the veal pieces until browned on all sides. Add onions or shallots and cook for 2 more minutes.

3 Add drained peas, carrots, stock, thyme and mace, making sure the cooker is no more than half full. Bring to high pressure and cook for 15 minutes. Reduce pressure with cold water.

4 Meanwhile, put rice, water and salt into a saucepan, bring to the boil and stir once. Reduce heat to simmer, cover and cook for 15 minutes, or until rice is tender and liquid absorbed.

5 Add a little water to the cornflour and mix into the veal mixture. Bring to the boil, stirring and cooking for 2–3 minutes in the open pan until thickened.

6 Check seasoning and serve over a bed of rice.

Creamy veal

cooking time: 15 minutes
pressure: high

you will need for 4 servings:

METRIC/IMPERIAL

575 g/1¼ lb stewing veal	1 (43-g/1½-oz) packet
2 tablespoons pure corn	chicken soup
oil	600 ml/1 pint water
4 carrots, sliced	100 g/4 oz peas

1 Trim the veal and cut into cubes. Heat the oil in the cooker with the trivet removed and sauté the veal and carrots until lightly browned.

2 Add the chicken soup mix and water and bring to the boil, stirring all the time, then stir in the peas. Making sure the cooker is no more than half full, bring to high pressure and cook for 15 minutes.

3 Reduce pressure at room temperature. Serve with rice or buttered noodles.

Bacon stew with peppers

cooking time: 15 minutes
pressure: high

you will need for 4 servings:

METRIC/IMPERIAL

575-g/1¼-lb vacuum-	freshly ground pepper
packed bacon joint	1 (396-g/14-oz) can peeled
1 tablespoon oil	tomatoes
100 g/4 oz onion, chopped	150 ml/¼ pint water
1 small green pepper	½ teaspoon dried
cut into dice	marjoram
2 cloves garlic, crushed	1½ tablespoons flour

1 Remove the bacon joint from all the wrapping and cut the bacon into 2·5-cm/1-inch cubes.

2 Put the oil in the cooker with the trivet removed and add the bacon, onion, pepper, garlic, ground pepper, tomatoes, water and marjoram.

ring to high pressure and cook for 15 minutes.
Reduce pressure at room temperature.
Blend the flour with water, add some of the hot
liquid and stir it into the stew. Bring to the boil,
stirring: cook gently for 2 minutes to thicken.
Serve with plain boiled rice.

Bacon and haricot hotpot

cooking time: 20 minutes
pressure: high

you will need for 4 servings:

METRIC/IMPERIAL

100 g/4 oz dried haricot beans	I stick celery, sliced thickly
450-g/1-lb piece of lean collar or gammon slipper	I (432-g/15¼-oz) can tomato soup
I tablespoon corn oil	I teaspoon mixed herbs
I medium onion, cut into quarters	pepper

Cover the beans with boiling water and leave to soak
for 30 minutes.
Remove the rind from the bacon and cut into cubes.
Put it in the cooker with the trivet removed, cover
with cold water, bring to the boil, then throw the
water away. Wash the cooker.
Heat the oil in the cooker with the trivet removed,
add the onion and stir round. Add the remaining
ingredients, including the drained bacon and beans,
and stir round.
Bring to high pressure and cook for 20 minutes.
Reduce pressure at room temperature.
Serve with potatoes, which could be cooked on the
trivet in separators for the last 5 minutes of the
cooking time.

Variation:

If a small (198-g/7-oz) can of sweet corn with its
juice is added to the hotpot, the dish could serve 5
people.

Red bean and ham stew

cooking time: 40 minutes
pressure: high

you will need for 5–6 servings:

METRIC/IMPERIAL

225 g/8 oz red kidney beans	600 ml/1 pint water
I gammon shank	2 bay leaves
25 g/1 oz butter	pepper
225 g/8 oz onion, chopped	½ teaspoon grated nutmeg
I (396-g/14-oz) can peeled tomatoes	

Place the beans in a bowl, cover with boiling water
and leave for 30 minutes.

2 Put the shank in the cooker with the trivet removed,
and bring slowly to the boil. Pour away the water and
remove any scum.
3 Return shank to the cooker, and half fill it with cold
water. Bring to high pressure and cook for 20
minutes. Reduce pressure at room temperature.
Throw the stock away.
4 Remove the rind from the shank and cut the meat off
the bone. Cut the meat into dice. The meat nearest
the bone may not be cooked through, but cut it off
anyway.
5 Wash the cooker. Melt the butter in the cooker with
the trivet removed, put in the onion and cook for 5
minutes. Add the tomatoes, water, bay leaves,
pepper, nutmeg and drained beans.
6 Return the meat to the pan, with the bone, if the
cooker is large: otherwise make sure the cooker is no
more than half full. Bring to high pressure and cook
for 20 minutes. Reduce pressure at room temperature.
7 Delicious served with garlic bread or with plain
boiled rice.

Variations:

a If garlic bread is not being served, a garlic clove can
be added, and a little tomato purée.
b Instead of the nutmeg use ½ teaspoon coriander and
½ teaspoon cumin seed.

● Hint:
If the cooker is not a large one and will not take a
gammon shank, use a gammon slipper instead.

Bacon medley

cooking time: 20 minutes
pressure: high

you will need for 4–5 servings:

METRIC/IMPERIAL

50 g/2 oz pearl barley	225 g/8 oz carrot
450 g/1 lb lean slipper or collar	2 sticks celery
I tablespoon oil	600 ml/1 pint stock
I 75 g/6 oz onion, chopped	bouquet garni
	pepper
I medium parsnip, peeled and sliced	chopped parsley (optional)
225 g/8 oz turnip, peeled and diced	

1 Put the pearl barley in a bowl and cover with boiling
water.
2 Remove the rind from the bacon and cut the meat
into 1-cm/½-inch cubes. Place it in a saucepan and
bring slowly to the boil, then throw the water away.
3 Heat the oil in the cooker with the trivet removed,
add the onion and stir round. Put in the remaining
ingredients, drain the pearl barley and add with the
bacon and a little pepper, making sure the cooker is
no more than half full.

4 Bring to high pressure and cook for 20 minutes. Reduce pressure at room temperature.
5 If liked, stir in a little chopped parsley before serving.

Variation:
½ teaspoon dried thyme would give added flavour.

Bacon casserole

cooking time: 17 minutes
pressure: high

you will need for 4 servings:

METRIC/IMPERIAL

1-kg/2-lb gammon slipper joint	1 onion, chopped
300 ml/½ pint chicken stock, made with ½ chicken stock cube	1 (227-g/8-oz) can peeled tomatoes
bouquet garni	225 g/8 oz potatoes, peeled and diced
	pepper

1 Remove rind from the bacon and cut the meat into cubes. Place in the cooker with the trivet removed, cover with cold water and bring slowly to the boil. Throw away the water.
2 Add the stock to the cooker with the bacon and bouquet garni. Bring to high pressure and cook for 10 minutes.
3 Reduce pressure with cold water, add the remaining ingredients. Return to high pressure and cook for 7 minutes.
4 Reduce pressure with cold water.

Variations:
a If extra bulk is required, stir in a well-drained 213-g/ 7½-oz can of butter beans after cooking, and just heat through.
b Crushed garlic would give this dish quite a kick.

Bacon à la crème

cooking time: 20 minutes
pressure: high

you will need for 4 servings:

METRIC/IMPERIAL

675-g/1½-lb gammon slipper joint	freshly ground pepper
300 ml/½ pint dry cider	1 (142-ml/5-fl oz) carton double cream
2 medium leeks, washed and sliced	1 tablespoon cornflour
4 cloves	1 teaspoon made English mustard
50 g/2 oz seedless raisins	

to garnish:
chopped parsley

1 Remove rind from the slipper and cut meat into 2-cm/1-inch cubes.
2 Place in the cooker with the trivet removed, cover with cold water and bring slowly to the boil. Pour the water away and rinse the bacon.

3 Wash the cooker, replace the meat, add the cider, sliced leeks, cloves, raisins and freshly ground pepper. Bring to high pressure and cook for 20 minutes. Reduce pressure at room temperature.
4 Blend the cornflour with a little of the cream and stir in the remainder. Add to the bacon with the mustard. Heat gently, stirring, until mixture thickens.
5 Serve sprinkled with parsley and mashed potatoes.

Variations:
a Use half stock and white wine instead of cider.
b Use a Meux mustard instead of the English mustard.
c Instead of cider use 150 ml/¼ pint stock, 1 (227-g/8-oz) can peeled tomatoes and 2 teaspoons tomato purée. Half a teaspoon dried marjoram could be an optional ingredient.

Bacon and bean hotpot

cooking time: 20 minutes
pressure: high

you will need for 4 servings:

METRIC/IMPERIAL

100 g/4 oz dried haricot beans	2 tablespoons flour
675-g/1½-lb smoked Danish collar joint	pepper
	1 (396-g/14-oz) can peeled tomatoes
25 g/1 oz butter	1 clove garlic, crushed
100 g/4 oz onion, sliced	300 ml/½ pint chicken stock
100 g/4 oz celery sticks, sliced	bay leaf

1 Cover the dried beans with boiling water and leave to soak for 1 hour.
2 Remove the rind and some fat from the bacon, and cut the meat into 2-cm/1-inch cubes.
3 Place the bacon in the cooker with the trivet removed, cover with cold water and bring slowly to the boil. Throw the water away.
4 Wash the cooker, melt the butter in the cooker with the trivet removed, add the bacon, onion, celery, stir in the flour and some pepper. Add the tomatoes, garlic, stock and bay leaf.
5 Stir round, then add the beans, well drained. Bring to high pressure and cook for 20 minutes. Reduce pressure at room temperature.
6 Serve with jacket or mashed potatoes.

Variation:
Instead of soaking and using dried beans, add (447-g/15¾-oz) can baked beans after reducing pressure. Just heat through in the open cooker.

● **Hint:**
A vacuum-packed rindless bacon joint could also be used. Remove from the bag and cut into cubes: no blanching would be necessary.

Barbecued bacon and sweet corn

cooking time: 15 minutes
pressure: high

you will need for 4 servings:

METRIC/IMPERIAL
575-g/1¼-lb vacuum-packed bacon joint
1 (376-g/13¼-oz) can barbecue Cook-In-Sauce

1 (198-g/7-oz) can sweet corn

Remove the bacon from the wrappings and cut the meat in strips about 1 by 5 cm/½ by 2 inches long. Place the bacon and sauce in the cooker with the trivet removed. Drain and add the sweet corn. Stir round.
Bring to high pressure and cook for 15 minutes. Reduce pressure with cold water.
Serve with noodles or mashed potato.

Variation:
Use a tomato and onion Cook-In-Sauce.

Parsley stuffed hearts

cooking time: 30 minutes
pressure: high

you will need for 4 servings:

METRIC/IMPERIAL
5 pig's hearts or 675 g/ 1½ lb lamb's hearts
25 g/1 oz parsley sprigs
2 tablespoons oil

450 ml/¾ pint stock, or water and 1 stock cube
salt and pepper
1 tablespoon cornflour

Wash the hearts and cut out the core, leaving the hearts whole. Stuff each with parsley and either sew up the tops or close them with skewers.
Heat the oil in the cooker with the trivet removed and lightly brown the hearts all over. Add the stock, salt and pepper. Bring to high pressure and cook for 30 minutes.
Reduce pressure at room temperature. Remove the meat, pull out the string or skewers and keep hot.
Blend the cornflour with a little water, add some hot stock and return it to the cooker. Cook for 2 minutes to thicken.
Pour the sauce over the hearts and serve with mashed potatoes and a green vegetable.

Variations:
Stir 1 tablespoon tomato purée into the sauce.
Add 1 tablespoon of sherry and ¼ teaspoon of dried mixed herbs.
Using 1½ tablespoons cornflour, blend into 150 ml/ ¼ pint double cream. Stir into the liquor in the cooker, bring to the boil to thicken.

Hearts in red wine

cooking time: 25 minutes
pressure: high

you will need for 4 servings:

METRIC/IMPERIAL
450 g/1 lb lamb's hearts
1 tablespoon oil
100 g/4 oz button mushrooms, washed

1 (376-g/13¼-oz) can red wine
Cook-In-Sauce
2 tablespoons water

1 Remove core and any excess fat from the hearts and wash them. Cut into strips.
2 Put the oil in the cooker with the trivet removed, add the hearts and stir round. Add the mushrooms, sauce and water, stir round and break down the sauce.
3 Bring to high pressure and cook for 25 minutes. Reduce pressure at room temperature.
4 Serve with noodles.

Variation:
Open cooker 8 minutes before the end of cooking time. Add sliced potatoes in separator, cover and place on the trivet: return to high pressure and cook for 8 minutes. Serve the potato mashed.

Casseroled hearts

cooking time: 20 minutes
pressure: high

you will need for 4 servings:

METRIC/IMPERIAL
6 lamb's hearts
2 tablespoons oil
1 onion, chopped
100 g/4 oz carrots, sliced
100 g/4 oz button mushrooms

2 tablespoons oxtail soup mix
300 ml/½ pint water

1 Remove the core and veins from the hearts and wash them. Drain and dry the hearts on kitchen paper. Cut them into fairly thick slices.
2 Heat the oil in the cooker with the trivet removed, add the hearts and onion, stir round and cook for a few minutes.
3 Stir in the carrots, mushrooms, soup mix and water. Bring to the boil in the open cooker and stir well.
4 Bring to high pressure and cook for 20 minutes. Reduce pressure with cold water.

Variation:
Cook for 15 minutes, reduce pressure, place prepared vegetables in the separators. Place the trivet on top of the hearts, then the separators. Return to high pressure and cook for 5 minutes.

Kidneys à la Midway

cooking time: 7 minutes
pressure: high

you will need for 4 servings:

METRIC/IMPERIAL
8–10 lamb's kidneys	1 (396-g/14-oz) can peeled
25 g/1 oz butter or	tomatoes
margarine	150 ml/¼ pint beef stock
1 medium onion, sliced	salt and pepper
2 carrots, sliced	1 teaspoon sugar
100 g/4 oz button	bay leaf
mushrooms, cut in	½ teaspoon dried thyme
quarters	1 tablespoon plain flour

1 Prepare the kidneys; remove skin, halve and cut out the core with a pair of scissors.
2 Heat the butter or margarine in the cooker with the trivet removed, put in the onion and carrots and cook gently to lightly brown. Add the kidneys and stir round to seal in the juices.
3 Add the remaining ingredients, except the flour, making sure the cooker is no more than half full. Bring to high pressure and cook for 7 minutes. Reduce the pressure with cold water.
4 Blend the flour with water, add some of the hot liquid and return it to the pan, stirring. Bring to the boil, reduce heat and cook for 1 minute to thicken.

Kidney casserole

cooking time: 7 minutes
pressure: high

you will need for 4 servings:

METRIC/IMPERIAL
25 g/1 oz butter or	1 teaspoon curry powder
margarine	300 ml/½ pint beef stock
2 rashers streaky bacon	2 teaspoons
1 large onion, sliced	Worcestershire sauce
½ small green pepper,	1 teaspoon sugar
deseeded and dried	1 tablespoon tomato purée
1 small clove garlic,	salt and pepper
crushed	2 tablespoons plain flour
8 lamb's kidneys, halved	
and cored	

1 Put the butter or margarine in the cooker with the trivet removed, add the bacon, onion, pepper and garlic, stir round and cook gently for 5 minutes.
2 Prepare the kidneys (see above), add them to the pan, stir round and cook for 2 minutes. Stir in the curry powder, stock, Worcestershire sauce, sugar, tomato purée, salt and pepper, making sure the cooker is no more than half full.
3 Bring to high pressure and cook for 7 minutes. Reduce pressure at room temperature.
4 Blend the flour with a little water, stir into the kidneys, bring to the boil, stirring, then reduce the heat and cook for 2 minutes until thickened.
5 Serve with rice and a green salad.

Tripe provençale

cooking time: 15 minutes
pressure: high

you will need for 3–4 servings:

METRIC/IMPERIAL
675 g/1½ lb dressed tripe	100 g/4 oz green pepper,
2 onions, peeled and cut	deseeded
into quarters	25 g/1 oz plain flour
40 g/1½ oz butter or	1 (396-g/14-oz) can peeled
margarine	tomatoes
1 teaspoon oil	salt and pepper
1 clove garlic	

to garnish:
chopped parsley

1 Wash the tripe and cut into 5-cm/2-inch pieces.
2 Place in the open cooker with the trivet removed with sufficient cold water to cover and bring just to the boil.
3 Discard the water and repeat the process, adding a little of the onion if liked. Make sure the cooker is no more than half full. Bring to high pressure and cook for 15 minutes.
4 Reduce pressure at room temperature. Drain off the liquid and put aside the tripe.
5 Melt the butter or margarine and oil in the open cooker. Put in the remaining onion and garlic and cook gently for a few minutes. Add the pepper, cut into chunky pieces.
6 Toss the tripe in the flour and add to the pan with the tomatoes, salt and pepper. Cook gently until the flour thickens and the tomato liquid is reduced a little.
7 Serve sprinkled with the chopped parsley with mashed potato.

Variation:
Replace the green pepper with 1 tablespoon curry powder. Add 1 teaspoon tomato purée, a pinch of sugar and a few sultanas.

Braised liver with dumplings

cooking time: 4 minutes
pressure: high

you will need for 4 servings:

METRIC/IMPERIAL
25 g/1 oz dripping or lard	2 carrots
1 large onion	1 small turnip
100 g/4 oz streaky bacon	2 beef stock cubes or 2
450 g/1 lb lamb's liver,	teaspoons beef stock
sliced	powder
25 g/1 oz plain flour	300 ml/½ pint water

for dumplings:
100 g/4 oz self-raising flour	½ teaspoon dried mixed
50 g/2 oz shredded suet	herbs
salt and pepper	4 tablespoons water

1 Melt the dripping in the cooker with the trivet removed, add the onion, cook for 5 minutes.

2 Remove the rind, cut the bacon in pieces, add it to the onion and cook for 2 minutes.

3 Coat the liver with flour, place it in the cooker and fry quickly on each side.

4 Put in the vegetables, sprinkle in the stock cubes or powder, add the water. Bring to high pressure and cook for 4 minutes. Reduce pressure at room temperature.

5 Meanwhile, place all the dumpling ingredients in a bowl and mix with enough water to give a soft dough. Use a little flour to shape the dumplings into eight pieces.

6 Return the open cooker to the heat, bring to the boil, add the dumplings, cover with a large plate and simmer for 10 minutes.

Variation:
Use parsley instead of herbs in the dumplings.

Liver and vegetable casserole

cooking time: 15 minutes
pressure: high

you will need for 4 servings:

METRIC/IMPERIAL	
675 g/1½ lb ox liver	25 g/1 oz dried mixed
150 ml/¼ pint milk	vegetables
2 tablespoons oil	salt and pepper
100 g/4 oz streaky bacon,	1 tablespoon tomato purée
rind removed, chopped	3 tablespoons plain flour
600 ml/1 pint beef stock	

1 Cut the liver in slices, put in a deep plate and cover with milk. Leave on one side for 10 minutes, then drain and dry it on kitchen paper.

2 Put the oil in the cooker with the trivet removed, add the liver and the bacon and fry gently.

3 Stir in the stock, vegetables, salt, pepper and tomato purée. Bring to high pressure and cook for 15 minutes. Reduce pressure at room temperature.

4 Blend the flour with a little water, add some of the hot stock, return it to the cooker, bring to the boil, stirring, and cook for 3 minutes until thickened.

Oxtail with olives

cooking time: 40 minutes
pressure: high

you will need for 3–4 servings:

METRIC/IMPERIAL	
1 tablespoon oil	175 g/6 oz carrots, sliced
1 kg/2 lb oxtail	fairly thick
300 ml/½ pint dry cider	2 medium sticks celery,
150 ml/¼ pint beef stock	cut in 2-cm/1-inch
salt and pepper	lengths
bay leaf	9 pimento-stuffed olives
225 g/8 oz button onions,	2 tablespoons plain flour
peeled but left whole	

to garnish:
chopped parsley

1 Heat the oil in the cooker with the trivet removed, add the oxtail and lightly brown all over. Add the cider, stock, salt, pepper and bay leaf.

2 Bring to high pressure and cook for 30 minutes. Reduce pressure with cold water. Add the onions, carrots, celery and olives.

3 Return to high pressure and cook for a further 10 minutes. Reduce pressure at room temperature. Lift out the oxtail on to a plate and when cool enough remove the meat from the bones.

4 Place the stew in a dish and leave overnight in a cold place for the fat to settle.

5 Remove some of the fat and return the stew to a pan. Blend the flour with a little water, pour into the pan and heat gently, stirring until thickened, then cook for 2 minutes.

6 Garnish with chopped parsley and serve with mashed potato.

Variations:
a Use half parsnips and half carrot.
b Instead of cider use a light beef stock.
c A tablespoon of tomato purée could be added.

Oxtail stew

cooking time: 40 minutes
pressure: high

you will need for 4 servings:

METRIC/IMPERIAL	
1 oxtail, jointed	bouquet garni
2 tablespoons flour	450 ml/¾ pint beef stock
salt and pepper	150 ml/¼ pint dry red
1 tablespoon oil	wine
3 onions, sliced	1 tablespoon tomato purée
3 sticks celery, chopped	1 tablespoon
2 leeks, sliced	Worcestershire sauce
4 carrots, sliced	

1 Trim the excess fat from the pieces of oxtail. Season the flour with salt and pepper and use it to coat the pieces of oxtail.

2 Heat the oil in the open cooker with the trivet removed and sauté the oxtail until browned on both sides.

3 Add the prepared vegetables and sauté for a further 3–4 minutes. Add the bouquet garni, stock, wine and tomato purée blended with the Worcestershire sauce, making sure that the cooker is not more than half full.

4 Bring to high pressure and cook for 40 minutes. Allow the pressure to reduce at room temperature. Skim off the surplus fat by drawing a piece of kitchen paper across the surface.

5 Discard the bouquet garni, check the seasoning and thicken, if liked.

Variations:
a Use 600 ml/1 pint light ale instead of stock and wine.

b Use 450 ml/¾ pint beer instead of ale: omit leeks and use instead 1 (396-g/14-oz) can peeled tomatoes.

● **Hint:**
If convenient, it is a good idea to prepare this dish in advance, so that the fat can be easily skimmed off when cool.

Garlic sausage casserole

cooking time: 4 minutes
pressure: high

you will need for 4 servings:

METRIC/IMPERIAL

25 g/1 oz butter or margarine	225 g/8 oz garlic ring sausage, cut in 1-cm/½-inch slices
1 onion, sliced	300 ml/½ pint beef stock
225 g/8 oz carrots, sliced	2 bay leaves
450 g/1 lb cabbage, shredded	¼-½ teaspoon caraway seed (optional)
pepper	

1 Melt the butter in the cooker with the trivet removed, put in the onion and carrot, stir round and cook for a few minutes.
2 Add the remaining ingredients, including the caraway if liked, making sure the cooker is no more than half full. Bring to high pressure and cook for 4 minutes.
3 Reduce pressure with cold water. Serve with mashed potato.

Variations:
a Use frankfurters instead of garlic sausage.
b Sliced apple could be added to the cabbage.
c A little soured cream could be stirred in before serving.
d Add a little sugar and vinegar to the onion mixture.

● **Hint:**
If the cabbage is shredded too coarsely, the thick stalks may still be a bit crisp.

Poultry and Game

Pressure cooking is an ideal method for cooking older, tougher birds as the flesh remains moist. These can be made into delicious dishes in minutes.

Frozen poultry must be totally thawed before cooking.

To add variety to the dishes, water, wine, stock, cider, lager or beer may be used.

The cooker should never be more than half full when cooking poultry or game in stock or sauce.

To ensure even cooking only birds weighing up to 1·5 kg/3½ lb (including stuffing) should be used. The bird should fit easily into the cooker to ensure that the steam circulates, and avoid any blocking of the outlets.

When cooking poultry and game the cooking liquid may be water, red or white wine, dry cider or stock. The minimum amount of liquid required will depend on your type of cooker, but will be either 150 ml/¼ pint or 300 ml/½ pint for up to 20 minutes' cooking time.

Poultry or game	Cooking times at high pressure
Chicken	
Very young	
(poussin), halved	7 minutes
joints	4 minutes
Roasting, whole	5 minutes per half kilo/per lb
joints	5 minutes
Boiling, whole	10 minutes per half kilo/per lb
joints	10 minutes
Turkey, joints (whole turkeys are too large for pressure cookers)	10 minutes
Duck, whole	12–15 minutes per half kilo/per lb
joints	12 minutes
Hare, joints	40 minutes
Rabbit, joints	15 minutes
Partridge, whole	7–10 minutes (depending on age)
joints	5–7 minutes (depending on age)
Pheasant, whole	7–10 minutes (depending on age)
joints	5–7 minutes (depending on age)
Venison	20 minutes
Grouse and pigeons (older birds)	10 minutes

Winter casserole

cooking time: 7 minutes
pressure: high

you will need for 4 servings:

METRIC/IMPERIAL
1·25-kg/2½-lb chicken
salt and pepper
65 g/2½ oz flour
50 g/2 oz butter
450 ml/¾ pint chicken
  stock

to garnish:
chopped parsley

2 tablespoons tomato
  purée
1 large onion, chopped
225 g/8 oz carrots, sliced
100 g/4 oz celery, sliced
1 clove garlic (optional)

1 Cut the chicken into joints and coat in the flour, seasoned with salt and pepper.
2 Melt the butter in the cooker with the trivet removed, add the chicken and fry gently to lightly brown. Stir in any remaining flour and gradually stir in the stock to break up the flour.
3 Add the tomato purée and stir to dissolve: add the onion, carrots, celery and garlic, if used, making sure the cooker is no more than half full. Bring to high pressure and cook for 7 minutes.
4 Reduce pressure at room temperature. Sprinkle with chopped parsley.

Braised lemon chicken

cooking time: 30 minutes
pressure: high

you will need for 4–6 servings:

METRIC/IMPERIAL
1·5-kg/3-lb chicken
juice of 1 lemon
2 teaspoons chicken stock
  powder

for stuffing:
1 (46-g/1⅗-oz) packet
  bread sauce mix
100 g/4 oz breadcrumbs
50 g/2 oz chopped suet
grated rind of 1 lemon

300 ml/½ pint water
1 tablespoon cornflour

1–2 teaspoons dried thyme
1 tablespoon chopped
  parsley
1 egg

1 Mix together the bread sauce mix, breadcrumbs, suet, lemon rind, thyme and parsley for the stuffing. Bind together with the egg and stuff the chicken.
2 Place the chicken in the cooker with the trivet removed, add the lemon juice, chicken stock powder and water, making sure the cooker is no more than half full. Bring to high pressure and cook for 30 minutes.
3 Reduce pressure at room temperature. Lift the chicken out on to the serving dish, and keep hot.
4 Blend the cornflour with a little cold water and stir into the stock. Bring to the boil, stirring all the time, and serve with the chicken.

French country chicken

cooking time: 10 minutes
pressure: high

you will need for 4 servings:

METRIC/IMPERIAL
4 chicken joints
2 tablespoons pure corn
  oil
4 rashers streaky bacon,
  chopped

1 (43-g/1½-oz) packet
French country
vegetable Soup
450 ml/¾ pint water

1 Skin the chicken joints. Heat the corn oil in the cooker with the trivet removed and sauté the chicken and bacon until lightly browned.
2 Add the French country vegetable soup mix and water and bring to the boil, stirring all the time. Make sure the cooker is no more than half full, then bring to high pressure and cook for 10 minutes.
3 Reduce pressure at room temperature. Serve with rice.

Paprika chicken casserole

cooking time: 7 minutes
pressure: high

you will need for 6–8 servings:

METRIC/IMPERIAL
2-kg/4½-lb chicken
3 tablespoons plain flour
salt and pepper
1 tablespoon oil
25 g/1 oz butter or
  margarine

1 onion, chopped
225 g/8 oz carrots, sliced
1–2 teaspoons paprika
25 g/1 oz stuffed olives,
  sliced

1 Divide the chicken into 8 joints. Season the flour and use to coat the chicken pieces: reserve the remainder.
2 Heat the oil, butter or margarine in the cooker with the trivet removed and fry the joints to lightly brown them. Transfer them to a plate. Add the onion and carrots, cook gently for 5 minutes without browning them.
3 Return the chicken to the cooker, sprinkle with paprika, 1–2 teaspoons according to taste, then pour in the chicken stock, making sure that the cooker is no more than half full. Bring to high pressure and cook for 7 minutes.
4 Reduce pressure under cold water. Transfer the chicken to a hot casserole: keep hot.
5 Blend the remaining flour with a little water to remove lumps, then a little hot stock. Add to the cooker with the peppers and olives, bring to the boil to thicken, then spoon over the chicken.
6 Either serve immediately with noodles or rice or place in a suitable container, seal, label and freeze.

Chicken cock-a-leekie

cooking time: 25 minutes
pressure: high

you will need for 4–6 servings:

METRIC/IMPERIAL

1·5-kg/3½-lb chicken	450 g/1 lb leeks, washed
bay leaf	and trimmed, sliced in
½ lemon	2-cm/1-inch lengths
25 g/1 oz butter or	1 onion, chopped
margarine	225 g/8 oz carrots, sliced
salt and pepper	25 g/1 oz plain flour

1 Place the giblets from the chicken in the cooker with the trivet removed with 450 ml/¾ pint of water. Bring to high pressure and cook for 10 minutes.
2 Reduce pressure at room temperature. Strain the stock into a measuring jug and make up to 450 ml/¾ pint with water if necessary. Discard the giblets.
3 Place the lemon and bay leaf in the body of the chicken. Melt the butter or margarine in the cooker, put in the chicken and lightly brown it all over.
4 Add the stock, salt and pepper making sure the cooker is no more than half full. Bring to high pressure and cook for 20 minutes. Reduce pressure at room temperature.
5 Add the leeks, onions and carrots: return to high pressure and cook for 5 minutes. Reduce pressure at room temperature.
6 Lift out the chicken on to a heated serving dish. Remove the vegetables with a slotted spoon and arrange round the dish. Keep hot.
7 Blend the flour with a little water to remove any lumps, add some hot stock, then pour it back into the cooker. Bring to the boil, stirring: reduce heat and simmer for 2 minutes to thicken.
8 Serve separately with the chicken.

Kentish chicken

cooking time: 7 minutes
pressure: high

you will need for 4 servings:

METRIC/IMPERIAL

4 chicken joints	225 g/8 oz button
15 g/½ oz butter or	mushrooms, washed
margarine	225 g/8 oz cooking apples,
175 g/6 oz onion, chopped	sliced
300 ml/½ pint dry cider	15 g/½ oz plain flour
salt and pepper	150 ml/¼ pint soured
1 teaspoon paprika	cream
1 tablespoon tomato purée	

1 Remove skin from the chicken joints, melt the butter or margarine in the cooker with the trivet removed and fry the chicken all over until lightly browned.
2 Transfer the chicken on to a plate and fry the onion until lightly browned. Add the cider, salt, pepper, paprika and tomato purée. Return the chicken to the pan, bring to high pressure and cook for 7 minutes.
3 Reduce pressure at room temperature, add the

mushrooms and apples. Return to high pressure and cook for 2 minutes.
4 Reduce pressure with cold water. Lift out the chicken, mushrooms and apples, put in a heated casserole dish and keep hot.
5 Blend flour with a little water, add some hot stock, pour into the cooker, bring to the boil, stirring, and cook for 2 minutes until thickened.
6 Pour in half the soured cream, just heat, taste and adjust seasoning if necessary. Pour over the chicken and serve.

Piquante chicken

cooking time: 7 minutes
pressure: high

you will need for 4 servings:

METRIC/IMPERIAL

25 g/1 oz butter or	salt and pepper
margarine	1 tablespoon demerara
4 quarter chicken joints	sugar
1 onion	½ teaspoon dried basil
1 (396-g/14-oz) can peeled	2 tablespoons orange
tomatoes	marmalade
150 ml/¼ pint water	
1 tablespoon	
Worcestershire sauce	

1 Melt the butter or margarine in the cooker with the trivet removed, brown the chicken on both sides. Remove it with a slotted spoon.
2 Add the onion to the pan and cook for a few minutes. Stir in the tomatoes, water, Worcestershire sauce, salt and pepper. Place the chicken joints on top.
3 Bring to high pressure and cook for 7 minutes. Reduce pressure at room temperature. Transfer the chicken to a heated serving dish and keep hot.
4 Add the remaining ingredients to the cooker, stir round and heat to reduce until fairly thick.
5 Spoon over the chicken and serve with rice and salad.

Coq au vin

cooking time: 20 minutes
pressure: high

you will need for 4 servings:

METRIC/IMPERIAL

25 g/1 oz butter or	300 ml/½ pint red wine
margarine	salt and pepper
175 g/6 oz button onions,	¼ teaspoon dried thyme
prepared but whole	bay leaf
4 rashers streaky bacon	1 tablespoon tomato purée
1·5-kg/3-lb chicken cut	pinch sugar
into 8 portions	*for beurre manie:*
2 tablespoons brandy	50 g/2 oz butter
100 g/4 oz button	50 g/2 oz plain flour
mushrooms	

to garnish:

chopped parsley	fried croûtons

Melt the butter or margarine in the cooker with the trivet removed, put in the onions and bacon and cook to lightly brown, about 5 minutes. Transfer with a slotted spoon on to a plate.

Add the chicken pieces and brown them gently all over. Warm the brandy in a spoon or small pan, then carefully set it alight and pour it, flaming, over the chicken in the cooker.

Return the bacon and the onions to the cooker. Add the mushrooms, wine, stock, salt, pepper, thyme and bay leaf, tomato purée and sugar. Bring to high pressure and cook for 20 minutes.

Reduce pressure at room temperature, and lift out the chicken.

Blend the butter and flour together for the beurre manié, add it in pieces to the pan, whisking it in to thicken the sauce. Bring to the boil, reduce heat and cook for 2 minutes to thicken.

Return the chicken to the pan and just reheat. Serve the chicken sprinkled with chopped parsley and croûtons arranged round the dish.

Moya's special chicken

cooking time: 7 minutes
pressure: high

you will need for 4 servings:

METRIC/IMPERIAL
40 g/1½ oz butter or margarine	300 ml/½ pint giblet stock, or water and stock cube
4 quarter chicken joints	1 tablespoon tomato purée
1 onion, chopped	2 tablespoons dry sherry
2 rashers bacon, chopped, with rind removed	¼ teaspoon dried mixed herbs
1 clove garlic (optional)	salt and pepper
100 g/4 oz button mushrooms	1 tablespoon plain flour

to garnish:
chopped parsley

1 Heat the butter or margarine in the cooker with the trivet removed and fry the chicken to lightly brown, turning once. Transfer on to a plate.

2 Put the onion, garlic and bacon into the cooker, stir round and cook until lightly browned.

3 Add the mushrooms, stock, tomato purée, sherry, herbs, salt and pepper, and return the chicken to the cooker. Bring to high pressure and cook for 7 minutes.

4 Reduce pressure with cold water. Arrange the chicken on a heated serving dish, and keep it hot.

5 Blend the flour with a little water, add some hot stock, pour it into the cooker, bring to the boil, stirring, and cook for 1 minute.

6 Spoon it over the chicken and sprinkle with chopped parsley.

Variations:

a Use marjoram or oregano instead of mixed herbs.
b Serve with croûtons.

Chicken casserole

cooking time: 7 minutes
pressure: high

you will need for 4 servings:

METRIC/IMPERIAL
1 tablespoon oil	1 tablespoon Worcestershire sauce
4 chicken joints	
2 leeks, cut in 2-cm/1-inch lengths	½ teaspoon dried mixed herbs
2 carrots, sliced in 1-cm/½-inch slices	salt and pepper
1 (227-g/8-oz) can peeled tomatoes	300 ml/½ pint chicken stock
	2 teaspoons cornflour

1 Heat the oil in the open cooker with the trivet removed, add the chicken joints and fry gently to brown.

2 Add the leeks, carrots, tomatoes, sauce, herbs, seasoning and stock, making sure the cooker is no more than half full.

3 Bring to high pressure and cook for 7 minutes. Reduce pressure at room temperature.

4 Blend the cornflour with a little water and add some hot stock. Return it to the cooker, stir round and cook for a few minutes to thicken.

● Hint:
If there is space, cook sprigs of cauliflower and potatoes at the same time in the separators on the trivet over the chicken.

Chicken and rice casserole

cooking time: 7 minutes
pressure: high

you will need for 4 servings:

METRIC/IMPERIAL
3 tablespoons corn oil	1 (396-g/14-oz) can peeled tomatoes
salt and pepper	
4 chicken joints	600 ml/1 pint chicken stock
2 sticks celery, sliced	
50 g/2 oz mushrooms, sliced	225 g/8 oz American long-grain rice

1 Heat the oil in the cooker with the trivet removed, fry the chicken joints until lightly browned, about 5 minutes.

2 Add the celery and mushrooms, fry for 1 minute, then put in the tomatoes, stock and seasoning.

3 Bring to the boil in the open cooker, add the rice and stir once. Bring to high pressure and cook for 7 minutes.

4 Reduce pressure with cold water, and serve in a heated dish with beans, or peas and carrots.

Chicken with chilli

cooking time: 7 minutes
pressure: high

you will need for 4 servings:

METRIC/IMPERIAL

I tablespoon oil	I–2 teaspoons chilli
4 chicken joints	powder
I large onion, chopped	450 ml/¾ pint chicken
I stick celery, sliced	stock
3 tablespoons tomato	salt
purée	I tablespoon plain flour
I teaspoon sugar	

1 Heat the oil in the cooker with the trivet removed, add the chicken joints and cook quickly to brown all over. Transfer them on to a plate.
2 Put in the onion and celery and fry for a few minutes to lightly brown.
3 Stir in the tomato purée, sugar, chilli powder (see hint below), stock and salt, making sure the cooker is no more than half full. Add the chicken joints.
4 Bring to high pressure and cook for 7 minutes. Reduce pressure at room temperature. Lift out the chicken and place on a heated serving dish to keep hot.
5 Blend the flour with a little water, add some hot liquor, then stir into the cooker. Bring to the boil, stirring, and cook for 1 minute to thicken.

Variations:

a Curry powder could be used instead of the chilli powder.
b Add redcurrant jelly or marmalade instead of the sugar.

● **Hint:**
Be careful when using the chilli powder – too much will ruin the dish, and different powders vary considerably in strength.

Rice-stuffed chicken

cooking time: 10 minutes per half kilo/per lb
pressure: high

you will need for 4–6 servings:

METRIC/IMPERIAL

I boiling chicken, not	50 g/2 oz raisins
more than 1·5 kg/3½ lb	25 g/I oz crystallised
I small onion, chopped	ginger, finely chopped
50 g/2 oz butter	salt and pepper
grated rind and juice of I	4 small whole onions
orange	8 whole carrots
¼ teaspoon mixed spice	flour for thickening
350 g/12 oz cooked	
American long-grain	
rice (100 g/4 oz	
uncooked rice and 300	
ml/½ pint stock)	

1 Wash and dry the chicken.

2 Fry onion in butter in a saucepan until soft, mix in the grated orange rind, mixed spice, orange juice, cooked rice, raisins, ginger and season lightly.
3 Use this mixture as a stuffing for the chicken and fasten securely. Weigh the bird in order to calculate cooking time.
4 Remove the trivet from the cooker, and put in the chicken with 450 ml/¾ pint water. Bring to the boil, add the vegetables, then cook at high pressure for 10 minutes per half kilo/per lb weight.
5 Reduce pressure at room temperature. Lift out the chicken, place on a heated serving plate and arrange the onions and carrots around it. Keep warm. Thicken the remaining liquid and serve as a sauce.

Choice chicken casserole

cooking time: 35 minutes (see method)
pressure: high

you will need for 4 servings:

METRIC/IMPERIAL

1·5-kg/3-lb chicken	175 g/6 oz button onions,
I tablespoon oil	peeled, but left whole
450 ml/¾ pint water	175 g/6 oz button
150 ml/¼ pint white wine	mushrooms, washed
2 bay leaves	225 g/8 oz long-grain rice
bouquet garni	2 canned red peppers
salt and pepper	

1 Remove giblets from the chicken. Heat the oil in the cooker with the trivet removed, put in the chicken, breast side down, and fry gently to brown.
2 Add the water, wine, bay leaves, bouquet garni, salt and pepper. Bring to high pressure and cook for 30 minutes, or 10 minutes per half kilo/per lb.
3 Reduce pressure with cold water, remove the chicken and keep hot. Remove bay leaves and bouquet garni, measure stock and make up 600 ml/1 pint if necessary.
4 Return to the cooker, add the onions and mushrooms: bring to the boil and stir in the rice, making sure the cooker is no more than half full. Bring to high pressure and cook for 5 minutes.
5 Reduce pressure with cold water. Stir in the red pepper.
6 Slice the chicken and serve with the rice. If liked, accompany with a parsley sauce.

Variations:

a Serve cold with the chicken removed from the bone and mixed in a mayonnaise. Add cooked peas, prawns and sweet corn to the rice: arrange on a dish with the chicken served on top. Decorate with wedges of tomato and watercress.
b Serve hot with the chicken removed from the bones, and stirred into a cream sauce.
c If the cooker is large enough, double the stock and rice and use a larger chicken to make a party dish.

Turkey casserole

cooking time: 10 minutes
pressure: high

you will need for 4 servings:

METRIC/IMPERIAL

I tablespoon oil	2 teaspoons stock powder
I kg/2 lb turkey thighs	150 ml/¼ pint water
I medium onion, chopped	2 teaspoons dried
I large clove garlic,	marjoram
crushed	salt and pepper
100 g/4 oz mushrooms,	15 g/½ oz flour
washed and quartered	15 g/½ oz butter
I (396-g/14-oz) can peeled	
tomatoes	

to garnish:
chopped parsley

Cut the turkey thighs in half, heat the oil in the cooker with the trivet removed and fry the thighs gently to lightly brown them all over.

Add the onion, garlic, mushrooms, tomatoes, stock powder, herbs, salt, pepper and water. Bring to high pressure and cook for 10 minutes.

Reduce pressure at room temperature, and transfer the turkey to a serving dish.

Blend the flour and butter together and add in small pieces to the liquor in the cooker. Mix in well to dissolve, bring to the boil and cook for 1 minute to thicken.

Spoon the sauce over the turkey and sprinkle with parsley.

Duck in sweet-sour sauce

cooking time: 20 minutes
pressure: high

you will need for 4 servings:

METRIC/IMPERIAL

I·75-kg/4-lb duck, cut	chicken stock
into 4 joints	2 tablespoons wine
2 tablespoons oil	vinegar
salt and pepper	I rounded tablespoon
2 large onions, sliced	brown sugar
¼ teaspoon ground cloves	I tablespoon cornflour
I (339-g/12-oz) can	
pineapple cubes	

Trim excess fat from the joints and prick the skin thoroughly with a skewer or fork. Sprinkle with salt and pepper.

Heat oil in a large frying pan and fry the joints until really brown and the skin side is crisp. Drain excess fat from the joints and place them in the pressure cooker with the trivet removed.

Add onions and cloves. Strain the juice from the pineapple and make up to 300 ml/½ pint with chicken stock: add it to the pan. Bring to high pressure and cook for 20 minutes.

Reduce pressure at room temperature. Lift the joints from the cooker and place on a hot serving dish. Skim off any surplus fat from the cooked liquid.

5 Mix the vinegar, sugar and cornflour to a smooth paste and stir into the cooker. Add the pineapple cubes. Bring to the boil, stirring, in the open pan and cook for 3 minutes.

6 Pour sauce over the duck and serve at once with plain boiled rice and peas.

Pigeon casserole

cooking time: 10 minutes
pressure: high

you will need for 4 servings:

METRIC/IMPERIAL

25 g/I oz butter	300 ml/½ pint stock
4 rashers streaky bacon,	salt and pepper
chopped	2 tablespoons cornflour
4 young pigeons, wiped	I tablespoon tomato purée
with a damp cloth	pinch sugar
225 g/8 oz button onions,	salt and pepper
peeled but left whole	
225 g/8 oz button	
mushrooms	

1 Melt the butter in the cooker with the trivet removed, put in the bacon and the pigeons and lightly brown them all over.

2 Add the onions, mushrooms, stock, salt and pepper. Bring to high pressure and cook for 10 minutes.

3 Reduce pressure at room temperature. Transfer the pigeons and onions with a slotted spoon into a casserole dish and keep hot.

4 Blend the cornflour, purée and sugar together with a little water, add some of the hot cooking liquor and return it to the cooker. Bring to the boil and cook for 1 minute until sauce thickens. Season to taste.

5 Pour the sauce over the pigeons in the casserole.

Variations:

a Use half pale ale and half stock.

b Half dry wine or dry vermouth and half stock would make a more exotic casserole.

c Cover with puff pastry for a pie.

Pheasant veronique

cooking time: 10 minutes
pressure: high

you will need for 2–4 servings:

METRIC/IMPERIAL

I or 2 pheasants,	salt and pepper
depending on size,	2 teaspoons arrowroot
prepared	4 tablespoons double
25 g/I oz butter	cream
300 ml/½ pint chicken	I teaspoon lemon juice
stock, or water and ½	100 g/4 oz green grapes,
stock cube	peeled and pipped

1 Remove any feathers from the pheasant and wipe the bird with a damp cloth.
2 Melt the butter in the cooker with the trivet removed, put in the pheasant and brown all over.
3 Add the stock to the cooker and salt and pepper. Bring to high pressure and cook for 10 minutes.
4 Reduce pressure at room temperature. Remove pheasant and cut into serving portions: keep hot.
5 Strain the liquor into a small saucepan. Blend the arrowroot with a little water and stir into the stock, bring to the boil and cook, stirring, until thickened.
6 Stir in the cream, lemon juice and grapes. Heat through, adjust seasoning and spoon over the pheasant. If liked, serve with fried bread croûtons.

Variations:
a Use half stock and half white wine instead of stock.
b Use 1 tablespoon Calvados instead of lemon juice: heat, set alight and pour over the pheasant before adding the stock.

Partridge with cabbage

cooking time: 10 minutes
pressure: high

you will need for 3–4 servings:

METRIC/IMPERIAL

2 small onions, peeled but whole	100 g/4 oz frankfurters, sliced
2 cloves	2 crushed juniper berries
2 partridges, prepared	salt and pepper
100 g/4 oz streaky bacon rashers, rind removed	300 ml/½ pint chicken stock, or water and ½
50 g/2 oz butter	stock cube
2 carrots, diced	
450 g/1 lb cabbage, washed and shredded	

1 Stud the onions with the cloves and place one in the body of each bird.
2 Cut the bacon in pieces, put it into the cooker with the trivet removed with the butter and carrots, heat and stir round to extract some of the fat from the bacon. Add the partridges and cook to brown all over.
3 Remove the partridges and put in the shredded cabbage. Stir round, add the remaining ingredients, and put the partridges back on top.
4 Bring to high pressure and cook for 10 minutes. Reduce pressure with cold water.
5 Serve the birds on the cabbage. The liquor may be thickened and served separately if liked.

Variation:
A tablespoon of vinegar and a few raisins added to the cabbage would give a sweet and sour effect.

Casseroled partridges

cooking time: 7–10 minutes depending on age
pressure: high

you will need for 2 servings:

METRIC/IMPERIAL

2 partridges, prepared	bouquet garni
25 g/1 oz butter	1 glass white wine
2 rashers streaky bacon, rind removed	450 ml/¾ pint stock
1 onion, sliced	salt and pepper
1 carrot, sliced	25 g/1 oz plain flour

to garnish:
crisps   watercress

1 Place the partridges in the cooker with the trivet removed, add the butter, the bacon cut into pieces and the onion. Cook gently to lightly brown the birds.
2 Add the carrot, bouquet garni, wine, stock, salt and pepper. Bring to high pressure and cook for 10 minutes.
3 Reduce pressure at room temperature. Take out the partridges and put aside on a serving dish to keep warm. Strain the stock into a saucepan.
4 Blend the flour with a little water, add some of the hot stock and return it to the pan. Bring to the boil, stirring, and cook for a few minutes until thickened.
5 Garnish the partridges with crisps and watercress. Serve the sauce separately.

Venison stew

cooking time: 20 minutes
pressure: high

you will need for 4–6 servings:

METRIC/IMPERIAL

675 g/1½ lb stewing venison, cut into pieces	1 tablespoon tomato purée
1 tablespoon oil	25 g/1 oz butter, softened
100 g/4 oz streaky bacon, cut into pieces	25 g/1 oz plain flour
100 g/4 oz button mushrooms	pinch sugar

for marinade:

2 carrots, sliced	2 tablespoons oil
1 onion, sliced	salt and freshly ground
2 cloves garlic, crushed	pepper
sprig of parsley	bay leaf
450 ml/¾ pint red wine	

1 Mix all the marinade ingredients together, add the venison and leave to stand for at least 6 hours: longer if a stronger game flavour is preferred.
2 Remove the meat from the marinade and discard the parsley. Heat the oil in the cooker with the trivet removed, put in the bacon and drained meat, fry fairly quickly.

3 Add the mushrooms, tomato purée and marinade: stir round. Bring to high pressure and cook for 20 minutes. Reduce pressure at room temperature.

4 Blend the butter and flour together and add in small pieces to the stew, stir to break down then bring slowly to the boil, stirring. Cook for 2 minutes until thickened.

5 Serve with plain boiled rice and a tossed green salad.

Hunter's rabbit casserole

cooking time: 15 minutes
pressure: high

you will need for 4 servings:

METRIC/IMPERIAL
450 g/1 lb rabbit pieces
100 g/4 oz streaky bacon rashers, rind removed
3 medium onions, sliced
2 large carrots, peeled and sliced

1 teaspoon dried mixed herbs
salt and pepper
300 ml/½ pint chicken stock

to garnish:
chopped parsley

1 Wipe the rabbit with a damp cloth: cut bacon into pieces.

2 Place these in the cooker with the trivet removed, add the onions, carrots, herbs, salt, pepper and stock, making sure the cooker is no more than half full.

3 Bring to high pressure and cook for 15 minutes, then reduce pressure at room temperature.

4 Serve sprinkled with the parsley.

Variation:

If liked, thicken the liquor and add 1 teaspoon tomato purée with a pinch of sugar.

Poacher's stew with dumplings

cooking time: 20 minutes
pressure: high

you will need for 4 servings:

METRIC/IMPERIAL
25 g/1 oz lard
1 large onion, chopped
2 sticks celery, chopped
1 kg/2 lb rabbit, cut into 8 pieces

25 g/1 oz flour
300 ml/½ pint brown ale
150 ml/¼ pint chicken stock

for dumplings:
4 rashers streaky bacon, rind removed
100 g/4 oz self-raising flour
¼ teaspoon salt

40 g/1½ oz shredded suet
1 tablespoon chopped parsley
3–4 tablespoons cold water

1 Melt the lard in the cooker with the trivet removed, put in the onion and celery and cook for 3 minutes.

2 Coat the rabbit in the flour, add to the cooker and fry to lightly brown the meat. Stir in the beer and stock.

3 Bring to high pressure and cook for 20 minutes, then reduce pressure at room temperature.

4 Meanwhile make the dumplings. Fry the bacon until crisp, drain on kitchen paper and chop finely.

5 Sieve the flour and salt, add suet, parsley and bacon, mix with the water to give a soft dough. Shape into 8 even-sized balls.

6 Remove lid, replace the cooker on the heat, bring to the boil, add the dumplings, cover with a large plate and simmer for 10 minutes.

To freeze:
The rabbit stew may be frozen. Prepare dumplings at the re-heating stage.

Rabbit casserole with prunes

cooking time: 15 minutes
pressure: high

you will need for 4 servings:

METRIC/IMPERIAL
100 g/4 oz dried prunes
50 g/2 oz butter
1 onion, chopped
4 rabbit joints
salt and pepper
300 ml/½ pint chicken stock, or water and stock cube

225 g/8 oz Cox's Orange Pippin apples, sliced
15 g/½ oz plain flour

1 Cover the prunes with boiling water and leave for 15 minutes. Drain well.

2 Melt the butter in the cooker with the trivet removed and lightly fry the onion for 5 minutes, then add rabbit joints and lightly brown.

3 Add the prunes, stock, salt and pepper. Bring to high pressure and cook for 15 minutes.

4 Reduce pressure with cold water, add the apples, bring to medium pressure and cook for 1 minute.

5 Reduce pressure at room temperature. Transfer the rabbit, apples and prunes with a slotted spoon to a heated serving dish.

6 Blend the flour with a little water, add some of the hot liquor, and return it to the pan, bring to the boil, stirring, and cook for 1 minute to thicken. Season to taste.

Variations:

a Use half pale ale and half water.

b A little chopped fresh sage would give the sauce a distinct flavour with a little tomato purée and cream.

Rabbit casserole with lager

cooking time: 17 minutes
pressure: high

you will need for 4–5 servings:

METRIC/IMPERIAL
1 rabbit
3 tablespoons plain flour
salt and pepper
50 g/2 oz butter or
  margarine
2 tablespoons oil
1 clove garlic (optional)
1 onion, chopped
150 g/5 oz streaky bacon
1 (275-ml/9·68-fl oz) can
  lager

2 teaspoons made English
  mustard
2 teaspoons French
  mustard
175 g/6 oz button
  mushrooms
salt and pepper
pinch sugar

1 Cut the rabbit into 6 joints, or ask the butcher to do it for you. Season the flour and use some of it to coat the rabbit pieces.
2 Heat 25 g/1 oz butter or margarine and the oil in the cooker with the trivet removed. Gently fry the rabbit until lightly browned.
3 Transfer the rabbit to a plate; add the onion, garlic and bacon to the cooker and fry gently to lightly brown. Pour in the lager and return the rabbit to the cooker.
4 Bring to high pressure and cook for 15 minutes. Reduce pressure at room temperature.
5 Remove rabbit from the pan. Blend in the two mustards. Blend the remaining butter or margarine with the reserved flour and whisk into the hot liquid.
6 Bring to the boil and cook for 2 minutes. Add the mushrooms. Taste and add sugar if necessary and adjust seasonings.
7 Return rabbit to the cooker. Bring to high pressure and cook for 2 minutes. Reduce pressure at room temperature.
8 Serve in a heated casserole.

Meat pudding and pie fillings

The choice of pie fillings could be endless but I have selected only a few.

The preparation and cooking time can be drastically reduced by cooking the meat beforehand, thus enabling the cook to prepare long-cook dishes during the week.

It is also possible to do larger amounts for freezing.

Steak and kidney pudding

cooking time: 15 minutes for filling; 15 minutes pre-steaming; 25 minutes for complete pudding
pressure: high for filling; low for complete pudding

you will need for 4 servings:

METRIC/IMPERIAL
350 g/12 oz chuck steak
100 g/4 oz kidney
seasoned flour
1 onion, chopped
100 g/4 oz mushrooms,
  sliced

bay leaf
300 ml/½ pint stock or
  water

for suet pastry:
225 g/8 oz self-raising flour
pinch salt
pinch mixed herbs

100 g/4 oz shredded suet
cold water to mix

1 Trim and cut the steak into cubes. Skin, core and slice the kidney. Toss the prepared steak and kidney in a little seasoned flour.
2 Put the meat in the cooker with the trivet removed and add the onion, mushrooms, bay leaf and stock, making sure that the cooker is not more than half full. Bring to high pressure and cook for 15 minutes. Allow the pressure to reduce at room temperature.
3 Meanwhile, make the suet pastry. Sieve the flour and salt into a bowl. Mix in the herbs and suet. Mix in sufficient cold water to form a soft dough. Roll out two-thirds and use to line a 1-litre/1½-pint greased pudding basin made of china, ovenproof glass or foil.
4 Allow the meat mixture to cool, remove the bay leaf and ladle into the lined basin with half the cooking liquid. Roll out the remaining dough to make a lid and use it to cover the pudding, dampening the edges for a secure seal. Cover securely with a piece of foil, making a pleat in the foil to allow room for the suet crust to rise during cooking.
5 Wash the pressure cooker, place the trivet in the base and pour in a scant 1·5 litres/2½ pints boiling water. Stand the basin on the trivet. Put the lid on the cooker and when steam escapes through the vent in the lid, lower the heat and steam, without the pressure weight, for 15 minutes. (This pre-steaming makes the suet pastry light). Increase the heat, bring to low pressure and cook for 25 minutes.
6 Allow the pressure to reduce at room temperature. Remove the basin from the cooker, take off the foil and serve from the basin, which may be wrapped in a napkin. Serve with the gravy remaining from cooking the meat.

Variations:
a Add a few oysters for a luxury old-fashioned pudding.
b Use 450 g/1 lb of diced uncooked bacon instead of steak and kidney.

● **Hint:**
Make a foil sling and place it under the basin before

putting it in the cooker. This makes it easier to lift the basin out.

Bacon pudding

cooking time: 55 minutes
pressure: high

you will need for 4 servings:

METRIC/IMPERIAL

450-g/1 lb lean piece of Danish gammon slipper	¼ teaspoon mixed herbs
50 g/2 oz onion, chopped	1 tablespoon plain flour
50 g/2 oz carrots, peeled and thinly sliced	200 ml/7 fl oz water

for suet pastry:

175 g/6 oz self-raising flour	pinch salt
75 g/3 oz prepared suet	7 tablespoons water

1 Remove the rind from the bacon and some of the fat. Cut the meat into 1-cm/½-inch cubes. Put the meat in the cooker and cover it with cold water. Bring to the boil, then pour away the water.
2 Cover the meat again with cold water, bring to high pressure and cook for 10 minutes. Reduce pressure with water, drain the meat and rinse under cold water. Dry on kitchen paper.
3 Put the meat in a bowl and mix in the onion, carrot, herbs and flour.
4 Make the pastry by mixing the flour, suet, salt and water together to make a soft dough. Knead lightly on a floured surface; cut off a quarter of the dough for the lid. Roll out the dough in a circle and use to line a 900-ml/1½-pint glass pudding basin.
5 Arrange the meat in the bowl and pour in the water (it may not be necessary to use all of it, depending on the shape of the bowl). Roll out remaining dough and seal on with a little water for the lid.
6 Cover with a double layer of greaseproof paper and tie down with string. Bring slowly to high pressure and cook for 45 minutes.
7 Reduce pressure at room temperature. Remove paper and string, and serve from the bowl, adding a little extra hot stock to the filling.

Variations:

a Add 50 g/2 oz button mushrooms instead of the carrots.
b Add 50 g/2 oz soaked prunes instead of the carrots.
c Use dried sage instead of the mixed herbs and 50 g/2 oz cooking apples instead of the carrots.

Hint:

If using a plastic or foil bowl, then reduce the cooking time by 5 minutes.

Chicken pie royale

cooking time: 20 minutes
pressure: high

you will need for 4–6 servings:

METRIC/IMPERIAL

1·25-kg/2¾-lb chicken	50 g/2 oz plain flour
600 ml/1 pint water	2 tablespoons sherry
1 onion stuck with 3 cloves	2 tablespoons top of milk
bay leaf	50 g/2 oz ham, cut into strips
50 g/2 oz butter or margarine	salt and pepper
1 small green pepper, cut into strips	1 (368-g/13-oz) packet frozen puff pastry
100 g/4 oz button mushrooms, sliced	

1 Remove the giblets from the body of the bird, take off their wrapping and put them in the cooker with the chicken. Add the water, onion and bay leaf.
2 Bring to high pressure and cook for 20 minutes. Reduce pressure at room temperature.
3 Allow the chicken to cool a little before stripping off the meat. Cut into pieces and reserve the stock.
4 Melt the butter in a saucepan, add the green pepper and mushrooms and cook for a few minutes. Transfer with a slotted spoon on to a plate.
6 Stir in the flour and work for 1 minute, gradually adding the reserved chicken stock, the sherry and the top of the milk. Bring to the boil, stirring, and work for 2 minutes until thickened.
7 Stir in the ham, peppers, mushrooms and chicken. Season to taste. Spoon into a 1-litre/2-pint pie dish. Roll out the puff pastry and cover the pie in the usual way.
8 Place in the oven, preheated to 220°C, 425°F, Gas Mark 7, and cook for 15 minutes. Reduce heat to 180°C, 350°F, Gas Mark 4, and continue cooking for 20 minutes.

Pork and kidney filling

cooking time: 20 minutes
pressure: high

you will need for 4 servings:

METRIC/IMPERIAL

450 g/1 lb boned blade of pork	salt and pepper
100 g/4 oz pig's kidneys	1 tablespoon Worcestershire sauce
1 tablespoon oil	300 ml/½ pint stock
2 medium onions, sliced	25 g/1 oz flour
100 g/4 oz button mushrooms	

1 Cut the pork into 2·5-cm/1-inch cubes and the kidney into 1-cm/½-inch cubes.
2 Heat the oil in the cooker with the trivet removed, add the pork, kidney and onions. Stir in the mushrooms, sauce and stock.

3 Bring to high pressure and cook for 20 minutes. Reduce pressure at room temperature.

4 Blend flour with a little water and add hot liquid; return to the pan and cook for a few minutes to thicken.

Variations:

a Use as a filling for a suet pudding using a 1-litre/1¾-pint basin (see Bacon Pudding, page 47).

b Put in a pie dish and cover with either puff or short-crust pastry.

c A little sliced apple and dried sage would be a tasty addition.

Liver and tomato filling

cooking time: 3 minutes
pressure: high

you will need for 4 servings:

METRIC/IMPERIAL	
450 g/1 lb lamb's liver	1 (227-g/8-oz) can peeled
2 tablespoons flour	tomatoes
1 tablespoon oil	1–2 tablespoons tomato
2 teaspoons marjoram or	purée
oregano	salt and pepper
1 medium onion, chopped	

1 Cut the liver into small pieces and toss it in flour.

2 Put the oil in the cooker with the trivet removed, add the liver and any loose flour. Stir in the remaining ingredients.

3 Bring to high pressure and cook for 3 minutes. Reduce pressure with cold water.

Variations:

a Use as a pudding with suet pastry (see Bacon pudding, page 47).

b Cover with puff or shortcrust pastry.

c Add chopped mushrooms and cover with mashed potato.

● Hint:

Liver cooked this way without the herbs, but with potatoes added, could be liquidised and used for baby food. Freeze in small pots the correct size for each portion.

Tavern pie

cooking time: 15 minutes
pressure: high

you will need for 4–6 servings:

METRIC/IMPERIAL	
2 tablespoons oil	2 tablespoons
2 large onions, chopped	Worcestershire sauce
450 g/1 lb stewing beef	salt and pepper
225 g/8 oz ox kidney	40 g/1½ oz plain flour
300 ml/½ pint brown ale	1 (368-g/13-oz) packet
150 ml/¼ pint water	frozen puff pastry,
¼ teaspoon dried thyme	thawed
rind of ½ orange, thinly	milk or beaten egg for
peeled	glazing

1 Heat the oil in the cooker with the trivet removed, put in the onions, stir round and cook slowly.

2 Cut the beef and kidney into 2-cm/1-inch cubes and add them to the cooker. Stir in the ale, water, thyme, orange rind, Worcestershire sauce and seasoning.

3 Bring to high pressure and cook for 15 minutes. Reduce pressure at room temperature.

4 Blend the flour with a little water, add some hot liquor and return to the cooker. Stir round and bring to the boil in the open cooker; cook for 2 minutes to thicken. Turn into a 1-litre/2-pint pie dish and allow to cool.

5 Roll out pastry and use to cover pie. Trim and decorate the edges.

6 Bake in a hot oven, 220°C, 425°F, Gas Mark 7, for about 25 minutes until the pastry is cooked and the meat is hot.

Rabbit pie

cooking time: 12 minutes
pressure: high

you will need for 4–6 servings:

METRIC/IMPERIAL	
450 g/1 lb boneless rabbit	2 tablespoons cornflour
meat, cut into pieces	3 tablespoons milk
1 onion, cut into quarters	2 tablespoons chopped
salt and pepper	parsley
300 ml/½ pint water	2 eggs, hard-boiled
bouquet garni	

for shortcrust pastry:

225 g/8 oz flour	pinch salt
100 g/4 oz fat	water

1 Place the rabbit in the cooker with the trivet removed, add the onion, salt, pepper, water and bouquet garni. Bring to high pressure and cook for 1 minutes.

2 Reduce pressure at room temperature, remove the bouquet garni. Blend the cornflour with the milk, add some hot liquid and stir into the cooker; bring to the boil, stirring, and cook for 1 minute to thicken.

3 Stir in the parsley, taste and adjust seasoning. Put on a plate to cool.

4 Make up the pastry in the usual way, divide it in two and use half to line a 20-cm/-8-inch ovenproof plate. Arrange rabbit in the centre, shell the eggs, slice and arrange them over the top. Damp the edges of the pastry.

5 Roll out remaining pastry and use it to cover the pie. Crimp the edges and brush with milk.

6 Cook in the centre of a preheated hot oven for 1 minutes at 220°C, 425°F, Gas Mark 7, then reduce heat to moderately hot 190°C, 375°F, Gas Mark for a further 15–20 minutes.

Variations:

a Instead of using cornflour to thicken, make a white sauce using 40 g/1½ oz butter or margarine and 40

1½ oz plain flour and adding the milk, then put in ½ teaspoon dried mixed herbs.

The addition of a few chopped up cooked bacon rashers gives a nice flavour.

Pigeon pie

cooking time: 7–10 minutes (see method)
pressure: high

you will need for 4–5 servings:

METRIC/IMPERIAL

2 pigeons, plucked and trussed	I small cooking apple, peeled
100 g/4 oz chuck steak	300 ml/½ pint beef stock
3 tablespoons plain flour	2 tablespoons sage and onion mix
salt and pepper	
3 tablespoons oil	I (212-g/7½-oz) packet frozen puff pastry, thawed
100 g/4 oz button onions, peeled but whole	

Cut the pigeons in quarters, removing any trussing string; cut away the thick backbone.

Cut the meat into cubes. Season the flour with salt and pepper and toss in the pigeon and meat.

Heat the oil in the open cooker with the trivet removed, add the pigeon, meat and onions, stir round and cook gently to lightly brown, for 5 minutes. Dice the apple and add with the stock.

Bring to high pressure and cook for 7–10 minutes – the longer time if the birds are known to be tough. Reduce pressure at room temperature.

Stir in the sage and onion stuffing mix. Allow to cool and turn into a 1-litre/2-pint pie dish. Cover with the pastry in the usual way.

Cook in a preheated hot oven 220°C, 425°F, Gas Mark 7, centre shelf for 20 minutes. Reduce heat to moderate 180°C, 350°F, Gas Mark 4 for a further 15–20 minutes.

Variations:

Mushrooms and half stock and red wine, with a few crushed juniper berries, would make a richer pie filling.

A few slices of cooked sausage would be cheaper than the chuck steak, although steak is considered to be traditional.

Steak and mushroom pie

cooking time: 15 minutes
pressure: high

you will need for 4 servings:

METRIC/IMPERIAL

675 g/1½ lb chuck steak	salt and pepper
50 g/2 oz button mushrooms, washed	2 tablespoons plain flour
100 g/4 oz button onions, peeled but left whole	I (212-g/7½-oz) packet frozen puff pastry, thawed
450 ml/¾ pint water or stock	

1 Cut the meat into cubes and place it in the cooker with the mushrooms, onions, water, salt and pepper.

2 Bring to high pressure and cook for 15 minutes. Reduce pressure at room temperature.

3 Blend the flour with a little water, add a little hot stock, stir into the meat, bring to the boil, stirring, and cook for 2 minutes until the sauce thickens. Taste and adjust seasoning.

4 Pour into a 1-litre/2-pint pie dish and allow to cool. Roll out the pastry and use to cover the pie dish. Brush with a little beaten egg or milk.

5 Bake in a preheated hot oven at 220°C, 425°F, Mark 7 for 15 minutes. Reduce temperature when the pastry has set to moderately hot 190°C, 375°F, Gas Mark 5 for a further 15–20 minutes.

Variations:

a Add a canned red pepper cut into dice when the meat is cooked.

b Stir in 1 tablespoon tomato ketchup and 1 teaspoon diced mixed herbs.

c Use beer and water instead of all water or stock.

d Red wine and water would also make a delicious stock; also add some tomato purée.

Continental Dishes

The following Continental dishes have been specially selected because they really lend themselves to pressure cooking and offer a considerable reduction in the cooking time normally required. The cooking time for the cassoulet, for example, has been reduced by hours.

I have tried to make this and the other recipes as traditional as possible, although it is not always easy to find the authentic ingredients.

Paella

cooking time: 5 minutes
pressure: high

you will need for 4 servings:

METRIC/IMPERIAL

4–8 chicken drumsticks, depending on size	I teaspoon turmeric
2 tablespoons vegetable oil	225 g/8 oz smoked cod or haddock, cubed
225 g/8 oz American long-grain rice	175 g/6 oz frozen peas
I large onion, sliced	I jar mussels, drained and rinsed in cold water
I clove garlic, crushed	salt and pepper
600 ml/I pint chicken stock	

1 Heat the oil in the cooker with the trivet removed, and fry the chicken drumsticks until slightly golden.
2 Add rice, onion and garlic and continue frying until the chicken is golden brown.
3 Add the stock, turmeric and smoked fish. Bring to high pressure and cook for 5 minutes. Reduce pressure immediately with cold water.
4 During pressure cooking, cook the peas separately and strain.
5 Add peas and mussels to the rice, mix thoroughly and allow to heat through before serving. Season as required.

Variations:

a 100 g/4 oz garlic sausage would be a tasty addition.
b For extra colour add a few whole prawns.

1 Melt the butter or margarine in the cooker with the trivet removed, put in the carrots, celery and onion. Stir round and cook for 5 minutes.
2 Remove the bone and excess fat from the lamb, and cut the meat into cubes about 2 cm/1 inch in size.
3 Add to the cooker, stir round and cook fairly quickly to seal in the juices. Add the water, salt and pepper. Bring to high pressure and cook for 15 minutes.
4 Reduce pressure at room temperature. Add the peas and return to high pressure and cook for 1 minute. Reduce pressure at room temperature.
5 Blend the egg yolks, flour and cream together, mixing well to break down any lumps. Add a little hot liquor, then pour back into the pan, stir round and heat gently until mixture thickens. Taste and adjust seasonings if necessary.

Tagliarini

cooking time: 5 minutes
pressure: high

you will need for 4 servings:

METRIC/IMPERIAL

2 tablespoons oil	1 (396-g/14-oz) can peeled
450 g/1 lb beef mince	tomatoes
2 cloves garlic, crushed	100 g/4 oz wholemeal
1 onion, chopped	pasta rings
1 medium green pepper, chopped	salt and pepper
1 (312-g/11-oz) can sweet corn	150 ml/¼ pint beef stock

to garnish:
Parmesan cheese

1 Heat the oil in the cooker with the trivet removed, put in the mince, onions, garlic and green pepper, stir round and cook for 2 minutes.
2 Add the sweet corn, tomatoes with their juice, pasta, salt and pepper, and stock. Bring to high pressure and cook for 5 minutes.
3 Reduce pressure at room temperature. Serve sprinkled with Parmesan cheese.

Greek lamb stew

cooking time: 15 minutes
pressure: high

you will need for 4 servings:

METRIC/IMPERIAL

25 g/1 oz butter or margarine	300 ml/½ pint water
	salt and pepper
175 g/6 oz carrots, sliced	100 g/4 oz frozen peas
175 g/6 oz celery, sliced	2 egg yolks
1 onion, cut into quarters	2 tablespoons flour
1·25-kg/2½-lb leg of lamb	2 tablespoons single cream
grated rind of 1 lemon	

Ossobuco

cooking time: 20 minutes
pressure: high

you will need for 4 servings:

METRIC/IMPERIAL

2 veal hocks, cut into 6 pieces	200 ml/7 fl oz dry white wine
1 tablespoon plain flour	1 (396-g/14-oz) can peeled
salt and pepper	tomatoes
50 g/2 oz butter	pinch sugar
2 carrots, chopped	sprig of rosemary
1 stick celery, sliced	225 g/8 oz long-grain rice
1 onion, chopped	600 ml/1 pint water
2 cloves garlic, crushed	1 teaspoon salt

to garnish:

2 tablespoons chopped parsley	grated rind of 1 lemon

1 Wipe the meat to remove any small splinters of bone. Season the flour and use to coat the pieces of veal.
2 Melt the butter in the cooker with the trivet removed. Put in the meat and brown it on both sides. Transfer it to a plate.
3 Add the carrot, celery, onion and garlic to the pan and cook gently for 10 minutes. Stir in the white wine, salt, pepper, tomatoes, sugar and rosemary.
4 Replace the meat, covering it with the sauce, and making sure that the cooker is no more than half full. Bring to high pressure and cook for 20 minutes.
5 Put the rice on to cook.
6 Reduce pressure at room temperature. Remove the meat and keep it hot; remove the rosemary. Reduce the sauce a little.
7 Drain the rice, place on a heated serving dish, put the meat on top and spoon the sauce over it. Mix the parsley and lemon together and sprinkle over the meat.

ot roasted chicken with parsley

cooking time: 20 minutes
pressure: high

you will need for 4 servings:

METRIC/IMPERIAL
(450-g/1-lb) chickens
0 g/4 oz butter
lt and pepper
g/1 oz parsley sprigs

150 ml/¼ pint water
150 ml/¼ pint double
cream
1 tablespoon cornflour

garnish:
mon slices
rigs of parsley

haw the chickens if necessary and remove the
blets.
often 50 g/2 oz of the butter, season with salt and
epper and add the parsley sprigs. Cream well
gether. Divide this butter and place half in the body
f each bird.
lelt the remaining butter in the cooker, with the
ivet removed, and brown the chickens all over. Add
e water. Bring to high pressure and cook for 20
inutes.
educe pressure at room temperature. Remove the
hickens, cut them in half lengthways and remove
e backbones. Reserve the parsley and keep the
hickens hot.
lend the cornflour with the cream, add to the stock
the pan and cook, stirring, until smooth. Stir in
e parsley and cook for 1 minute to thicken. Taste
nd adjust seasonings.
erve garnished with lemon and extra parsley sprigs.

Variation:
little crushed garlic added to the butter would give
dded flavour.

Ratatouille

cooking time: 4 minutes
pressure: high

you will need for 4–6 servings:

METRIC/IMPERIAL
onions, sliced
50 g/1 lb tomatoes,
skinned and chopped
courgettes, sliced
aubergines, sliced
red pepper, sliced

1 green pepper, sliced
2 tablespoons pure corn
oil
2 cloves garlic, crushed
salt and pepper
150 ml/¼ pint water

Prepare all the vegetables.
Heat the corn oil in the cooker with the trivet
removed and fry the garlic for 2 minutes.
Add the vegetables, seasoning to taste and mix well.
Pour in the water.
Bring to high pressure over a low heat and cook for
4 minutes. Reduce pressure with cold water.

Minestrone

cooking time: 10 minutes
pressure: high

you will need for 4–6 servings:

METRIC/IMPERIAL
2 tablespoons corn oil
1 carrot, chopped
2 sticks celery, chopped
1 onion, chopped
1 small turnip, chopped
1 potato, chopped
1 clove garlic, crushed
1 small leek, sliced
100 g/4 oz green cabbage,
finely shredded

2 large tomatoes, skinned
and chopped
50 g/2 oz short macaroni
bouquet garni
bay leaf
1 litre/1¾ pints beef or
ham stock
salt and black pepper

to garnish:
50 g/2 oz Parmesan
cheese, grated

1 Heat the oil in the cooker, with the trivet removed.
2 Put in all the prepared vegetables and, gently stirring,
cook for about 2 minutes.
3 Add the remaining ingredients, making sure the
cooker is no more than half full; stir, bring to high
pressure and cook for 10 minutes.
4 Reduce pressure at room temperature. Serve in
individual bowls with grated Parmesan cheese
sprinkled over each.

Stuffed veal rolls

cooking time: 10 minutes
pressure: high

you will need for 4 servings:

METRIC/IMPERIAL
4 veal escalopes
4 slices cooked ham
50 g/2 oz peanuts,
chopped
2 tablespoons chopped
parsley
2 tablespoons sultanas,
chopped

2 tablespoons grated
Parmesan cheese
25 g/1 oz butter
300 ml/½ pint white wine,
or chicken stock
1 rounded teaspoon
cornflour
salt and pepper

to garnish:
sprigs of parsley

1 Well flatten the escalopes and place the ham on top.
2 Mix the peanuts, parsley, sultanas and cheese together and spread over the ham. Roll up the escalopes and secure them with wooden cocktail sticks.
3 Melt the butter in the pressure cooker with the trivet
removed and fry the rolls till brown all over. Pour
off excess fat and add the wine or stock. Bring to high
pressure and cook for 10 minutes.
4 Reduce pressure at room temperature. Lift out the
rolls and put them on a hot serving dish.
5 Blend the cornflour to a smooth paste with a little
water and stir into the pan. Bring to the boil, stirring,
and cook for 2–3 minutes. Season to taste.

6 Pour the sauce over the rolls and garnish with parsley. Serve with a green vegetable and potatoes.

Chicken Italian

cooking time: 10 minutes
pressure: high

you will need for 4 servings:

METRIC/IMPERIAL
4 chicken joints	1 green pepper, cut into
2 tablespoons oil	strips
1 large onion, chopped	salt and pepper
450 g/1 lb fresh tomatoes,	100 g/4 oz ham, cut into
skinned and chopped	strips
1 clove garlic (optional)	150 ml/¼ pint chicken
4 tablespoons dry	stock
Vermouth	
½ teaspoon crushed	
rosemary	

1 Put the chicken joints and the oil in the cooker with the trivet removed. Fry the joints slowly until lightly browned.
2 Add the remaining ingredients. Bring to high pressure and cook for 10 minutes.
3 Reduce pressure at room temperature. Arrange the chicken on a dish and spoon sauce over it.

Cassoulet

cooking time: 20 minutes
pressure: high

you will need for 4 servings:

METRIC/IMPERIAL
350 g/12 oz haricot beans	225 g/8 oz garlic sausage
225 g/8 oz belly of pork,	50 g/2 oz lard or bacon fat
rind and any bone	2 onions, peeled but whole
removed	4 cloves
225-g/8-oz slice smoked	bouquet garni
collar of bacon, rind	salt and pepper
removed	2 carrots, peeled
175 g/6 oz lamb chump	4 cloves garlic, crushed
chops	600 ml/1 pint water
100 g/4 oz pork rind	

to garnish:
50 g/2 oz toasted breadcrumbs

1 Cover the beans with boiling water and leave to soak for 30 minutes.
2 Cut the belly of pork and bacon into 2-cm/1-inch slices and the lamb into pieces; cut the pork rind in half.
3 Melt the lard or bacon fat in the cooker with the trivet removed, add the pork, bacon, lamb and pork rind. Stir round and cook to lightly brown. Remove these meats with a slotted spoon and keep them on one side.
4 Cut the garlic sausage into thick slices and brown on all sides.

5 Return the meats to the cooker. Add the onions stuck with the cloves, the bouquet garni, carrots, garlic, water, salt and pepper. Bring to high pressure and cook for 20 minutes.
6 Reduce pressure at room temperature. Serve in a casserole, sprinkle the top with toasted breadcrumbs.

Variations:
a If available, pickled goose or a duck portion may be added as these are traditional ingredients.
b Three tomatoes, skinned and chopped, could be added or a small 227-g/8-oz can of peeled tomatoes with a little less stock.
c If a crusty top is preferred, place the casserole (making sure it is flameproof) under a moderate grill to brown the crumbs further.

Carefree (all-in-one cookery)

Take your pressure cooker away on a camping or caravanning holiday – it could prove to be your most useful piece of equipment. With perhaps only two burners and a pressure cooker, you can achieve quite ambitious dishes and be economical with the fuel.

These recipes have been devised so that all the ingredients are in the cooker together, or just require minimal accompaniments. The cooker can then be used to provide a sweet (see chapter on sweets and puddings).

● **Hints:**
a Do follow the cooking times carefully.
b Be adventurous. If, because of limited facilities, some ingredients are not available, try suitable alternatives.
c Ensure that you have the right sized cooker for the number of people to be fed.

Meat balls

cooking time: 8 minutes
pressure: high

you will need for 4–5 servings:

METRIC/IMPERIAL
225 g/8 oz beef mince	salt and pepper
225 g/8 oz veal mince	½ beaten egg
6 tablespoons sage and	a little lard or oil
onion stuffing mix	

for sauce:
1 (43-g/1½-oz) packet	1 tablespoon soured
mushroom soup	cream or yogurt
1 teaspoon tomato purée	pinch sugar

Mix the meats, stuffing mix, salt, pepper and egg together; shape into 20 balls.

Heat the fat or oil in a frying pan and fry the balls until nicely browned all over. Remove and drain on kitchen paper.

Make up the soup according to the directions on the packet but using only 450 ml/¾ pint water. Bring to the boil and cook to thicken; stir in the remaining sauce ingredients.

Place the meat balls in a soufflé dish that will fit into the cooker and pour the sauce over them. Cover with a double layer of foil and tie down.

Place the dish on the trivet with the minimum amount of water in the cooker. Bring to high pressure and cook for 8 minutes.

Reduce pressure at room temperature and serve with noodles or spaghetti.

Variations:

Make up a packet of stroganoff sauce instead of using dried mushroom soup.

Use a 298-g/10½-oz can of condensed tomato soup with half the amount of water; add yogurt or soured cream and a pinch of sugar. Extra tomato purée and garlic would add richness.

Make the balls as before but cook on a layer of cabbage, onion and canned tomatoes with the juice made up to 300 ml/½ pint with stock.

Use minced ham instead of beef.

Hint:

This dish can easily be prepared in the morning and finished off in the evening.

Sausage and bean stew

cooking time: 4 minutes
pressure: high

you will need for 4–6 servings:

METRIC/IMPERIAL
2 tablespoons corn oil
2 carrots, sliced
1 large onion, chopped
450 ml/¾ pint beef stock
1 (447-g/15¾-oz) can baked beans
1 tablespoon tomato ketchup

2 teaspoons strong made mustard
2–3 frankfurter sausages, depending on length
50 g/2 oz salami, diced

Put the oil, carrots and onion in the cooker with the trivet removed and cook for 5 minutes to lightly brown.

Add the stock, beans, ketchup and mustard, making sure the cooker is no more than half full. Bring to high pressure for 4 minutes.

Reduce pressure at room temperature. Add the prepared meats, stir round and heat through in the open pan.

Serve with thick slices of bread.

Bacon pilaff

cooking time: 6 minutes
pressure: high

you will need for 4 servings:

METRIC/IMPERIAL
75 g/3 oz butter
100 g/4 oz button mushrooms, washed
1 onion, chopped
2 sticks celery, sliced
1 green pepper, deseeded and cut into strips
225 g/8 oz long-grain rice

600 ml/1 pint chicken stock
salt and pepper
100 g/4 oz cooked peas
225 g/8 oz cooked bacon
25 g/1 oz sultanas
50 g/2 oz salted peanuts

1 Melt the butter in the cooker with the trivet removed, add the mushrooms and cook for 1 minute. Remove with a slotted spoon.

2 Add the onion, celery and pepper; stir round and cook for 1 minute.

3 Stir in the rice and cook for about 1 minute until transparent, stir in the stock, salt and pepper. Bring to the boil in the open cooker, making sure the cooker is no more than half full. Stir well before covering pan.

4 Bring to high pressure and cook for 6 minutes, keeping just at required pressure. Reduce pressure with cold water.

5 Stir in the remaining ingredients, heat through for a few minutes and adjust seasoning.

Bacon and potato stew

cooking time: 20 minutes
pressure: high

you will need for 4 servings:

METRIC/IMPERIAL
1-kg/2¼-lb vacuum-packed bacon joint
150 ml/¼ pint dry cider
150 ml/¼ pint water
¼ teaspoon dried thyme (optional)
1 medium onion, sliced

2 sticks celery, sliced
4 carrots, sliced
2 leeks, washed and sliced
pepper
450 g/1 lb potatoes, peeled and sliced

to garnish:
chopped parsley

1 Remove the joint from the wrappings and cut into 1-cm/½-inch cubes.

2 Put the meat in the cooker with the trivet removed, add the cider, water, thyme if used, onion, celery, carrots, leeks and pepper. Bring to high pressure and cook for 20 minutes.

3 Reduce pressure at room temperature. Add the potatoes, then bring to high pressure and cook for 5 minutes.

4 Serve sprinkled with chopped parsley.

Spiced pork and bean dinner

cooking time: 20 minutes
pressure: high

you will need for 4 servings:

METRIC/IMPERIAL

100 g/4 oz red kidney beans	¼ teaspoon ground coriander
450 g/1 lb lean belly of pork	¼ teaspoon cumin
2 tablespoons oil	450 ml/¾ pint chicken stock
1 leek, trimmed and washed	salt and pepper
2 tablespoons flour	225 g/8 oz frozen cut green beans
175 g/6 oz onion, cut into eighths	450 g/1 lb potatoes, peeled and thinly sliced
225 g/8 oz carrots, peeled and halved lengthways	

1 Cover the beans with boiling water and leave to soak for 30 minutes. Remove the rind and any bone from the pork belly and cut into 2-cm/1-inch pieces.
2 Heat the oil in the cooker with the trivet removed, add the belly and cook gently to extract some of the fat.
3 Cut the leeks into 2-cm/1-inch lengths and add to the cooker with the flour, onion, carrots, spices, stock, salt and pepper.
4 Drain the beans and add them too, stirring round to mix in the flour. Bring to high pressure and cook for 15 minutes.
5 Reduce pressure with cold water. Stir the casserole, and put the trivet in place. On this, put the potatoes and beans in perforated separators and add a little seasoning. Return to high pressure and cook for 5 minutes.
6 Reduce pressure with cold water and serve.

Curried minced beef

cooking time: 15 minutes
pressure: high

you will need for 4 servings:

METRIC/IMPERIAL

1 tablespoon oil	1 teaspoon sugar
450 g/1 lb beef mince	25 g/1 oz sultanas
1 medium onion, chopped	1 tablespoon chutney
1 tablespoon dried mixed peppers	300 ml/½ pint beef stock
¼–1 tablespoon curry powder	

1 Put the oil in the cooker with the trivet removed, add the mince and onion, stir round and cook for a few minutes.
2 Add the remaining ingredients, making sure the cooker is no more than half full. Bring to high pressure and cook for 15 minutes.
3 Reduce pressure at room temperature. Serve with

sliced banana, chutney, diced cucumber and redcurrant jelly.

Variations:

a Cook the mince for 10 minutes, then cook the rice the same way as for lamb curry.
b If liked, a small 227-g/8-oz can of peeled tomatoes could be added.

All-in-one stew

cooking time: 20 minutes
pressure: high

you will need for 6 servings:

METRIC/IMPERIAL

675 g/1½ lb lamb fillet	1 teaspoon beef stock powder
1 tablespoon oil	300 ml/½ pint water
175 g/6 oz onion, chopped	salt and pepper
2 medium carrots, sliced	350 g/12 oz small potatoes
2 sticks celery, sliced	1 clove garlic (optional)
2 (396-g/14-oz) cans peeled tomatoes	

to garnish:
chopped parsley

1 Cut the fillet into 2-cm/1-inch cubes. Heat the oil in the cooker with the trivet removed, put in the meat and fry fairly quickly to seal in the juices.
2 Add the onion, carrots, celery, tomatoes, water, stock powder, salt and pepper, making sure the cooker is no more than half full. Bring to high pressure and cook for 15 minutes.
3 Reduce pressure at room temperature. Cut the potatoes into chunks and add to the stew. Return to high pressure and cook for 5 minutes.
4 Reduce pressure with cold water. Sprinkle with chopped parsley and serve with chunks of bread.

Creamy chicken and rice

cooking time: 5 minutes
pressure: high

you will need for 4 servings:

METRIC/IMPERIAL

50 g/2 oz margarine	1 (298-g/10½-oz) can condensed cream of mushroom soup
1 large onion, sliced	
1 green pepper, sliced	2 tablespoons dry sherry
350 g/12 oz raw chicken, in bite-sized pieces	600 ml/1 pint chicken stock
225 g/8 oz American long-grain rice	salt and pepper

1 Melt the margarine in the cooker with the trivet removed, sauté the onion and pepper until just soft. Add the chicken and rice and sauté for a minute.
2 Add soup, sherry, stock, salt and pepper, bring to the boil in the open cooker and stir once, making sure the cooker is no more than half full.

Bring to high pressure and cook for 5 minutes.
Reduce pressure with cold water.
Serve the rice in a heated dish, accompanied by a tossed green salad.

Mexican beef with rice

cooking time: 5 minutes
pressure: high

you will need for 4 servings:

METRIC/IMPERIAL
I tablespoon corn oil	I½ teaspoons chilli powder
450 g/I lb minced beef	I tablespoon tomato purée
I onion, chopped	600 ml/I pint beef stock
I (432-g/15¼-oz) can red kidney beans	225 g/8 oz American long-grain rice
4 tomatoes, chopped	

Heat the oil in the cooker with the trivet removed, put in the mince and onion and fry until browned. Add the beans, tomatoes, chilli powder, tomato purée and stock.
Bring to the boil in the open cooker, add the rice and stir once, making sure the cooker is no more than half full. Bring to high pressure and cook for 5 minutes.
Reduce pressure with cold water. Serve the rice in a heated serving dish accompanied by a tossed salad.

Sausage risotto

cooking time: 5 minutes
pressure: high

you will need for 4 servings:

METRIC/IMPERIAL
8 pork sausages, thickly sliced	600 ml/I pint meat stock
50 g/2 oz dripping	I teaspoon crushed rosemary
100 g/4 oz mushrooms, sliced	¼ teaspoon ground ginger
I large onion, sliced	¼ teaspoon coarse black pepper
225 g/8 oz American long-grain rice	salt
	175 g/6 oz frozen peas

Heat the dripping in the cooker with the trivet removed, fry the sausages, mushrooms, onion and rice for 1 minute.
Add the stock and seasonings, bring to the boil in the open cooker and stir once, making sure the cooker is no more than half full. Bring to high pressure and cook for 5 minutes.
Cook the frozen peas separately.
Reduce pressure with cold water, strain the peas, stir into the rice and serve. If liked, serve with a tomato salad.

Kidneys in oxtail

cooking time: 7 minutes
pressure: high:

you will need for 4 servings:

METRIC/IMPERIAL
12 lamb's kidneys	I tablespoon tomato purée
50 g/2 oz butter or margarine	I (198-g/7-oz) can Mexicorn
½ (43-g/1½-oz) packet oxtail soup	pepper
300 ml/½ pint cold water	I (142-ml/5-fl oz) carton natural yogurt

1 Prepare the kidneys: halve, remove skin and cut out the core with a pair of scissors.
2 Melt the butter in the cooker with the trivet removed, put in the kidneys, stir round and cook for 5 minutes.
3 Sprinkle in the soup powder and gradually stir in the water. Bring to the boil, stirring.
4 Add the tomato purée and Mexicorn, including the juices; add a little pepper. Bring to high pressure and cook for 7 minutes.
5 Reduce pressure with cold water. Stir in the yogurt and just reheat. Serve with plain cooked rice.

Variations:

a Instead of using Mexicorn, add canned cut green beans and red peppers after reducing pressure; reheat.
b Baked beans could also be added instead of sweet corn. Serve with canned new potatoes.

Liver casserole

cooking time: 6 minutes
pressure: high

you will need for 4 servings:

METRIC/IMPERIAL
450 g/I lb ox liver in I piece	675 g/1½ lb potatoes, thickly sliced
little milk	350 g/12 oz onions, sliced
2 tablespoons seasoned flour	450 ml/¾ pint beef stock
3 tablespoons oil	2 tablespoons cornflour

1 Cut the liver into 5-cm/2-inch squares, put on a plate and pour some milk over it. Leave to stand for 10 minutes, turning the pieces.
2 Dry the liver on absorbent paper and dip it in seasoned flour.
3 Heat the oil in the cooker with the trivet removed, and fry the liver on both sides in the open cooker. Add the potatoes, onion and stock. Bring to high pressure and cook for 6 minutes.
4 Reduce pressure with cold water, transfer the liver and vegetables to a heated casserole and keep hot.
5 Blend the cornflour with a little water, add some of the hot stock, return to the cooker, stir round and bring to the boil. Cook for 1 minute to thicken.

6 Pour the sauce over the liver and vegetables and serve.

Variation:
As an extra vegetable, and to add colour, add a few sliced carrots.

Provençale lamb

cooking time: 20 minutes
pressure: high

you will need for 4 servings:

METRIC/IMPERIAL	
675-g/1½-lb neck of lamb	2 cloves garlic, crushed
1 large onion, sliced	salt and pepper
1 (396-g/14-oz) can peeled	300 ml/½ pint water
tomatoes	350 g/12 oz potatoes,
1 teaspoon stock powder	sliced

to garnish:
chopped parsley

1 Wipe the meat and remove any small pieces of bone. Place it in a single layer in the cooker with the trivet removed. Arrange the onion over the top, and pour the tomatoes over the meat, breaking up any large ones.
2 Sprinkle over it the stock powder, garlic, salt and pepper and add the water. Bring to high pressure and cook for 15 minutes.
3 Reduce pressure with cold water, arrange the potatoes over the surface and sprinkle them lightly with salt. Return to high pressure and cook for 5 minutes.
4 Reduce pressure at room temperature. Serve sprinkled with chopped parsley.

Bulk cooking

Depending on its size, using a pressure cooker for bulk cooking can be a great boon if you are a freezer owner or need to cater for large numbers. Concentrated soups, stews, casseroles and pie fillings can all be made in large quantities, divided and frozen in suitable dishes.

A lot of recipes in this book can also be adapted to give larger portions.

Fresh tomato soup

cooking time: 5 minutes
pressure: high

you will need for 8 servings:

METRIC/IMPERIAL	
4 rashers streaky bacon	1 teaspoon dried thyme
1 medium onion, chopped	salt and pepper
1 tablespoon oil	300 ml/½ pint chicken
1 kg/2 lb tomatoes, halved	stock
1 (425-g/15-oz) can peeled	
tomatoes	

1 Remove rind from the bacon and cut it into pieces.
2 Put the bacon, onion and oil in the cooker with the trivet removed and fry gently for 3 minutes.
3 Add the remaining ingredients, making sure the cooker is no more than half full. Bring to high pressure and cook for 5 minutes.
4 Reduce pressure at room temperature. Sieve or liquidise the soup.
5 Reheat and serve at once with a little fresh cream, or freeze in two 600-ml/1-pint portions.

Creamed artichoke soup

cooking time: 10 minutes
pressure: high

you will need for 8 servings:

METRIC/IMPERIAL	
50 g/2 oz butter or	600 ml/1 pint chicken
margarine	stock
1 medium onion, chopped	salt and pepper
1 kg/2 lb Jerusalem	
artichokes, peeled	

to serve:

600 ml/1 pint milk	little chopped parsley
4 tablespoons single cream	

1 Melt the butter in the cooker with the trivet removed, put in the onion and cook gently.
2 Cut up the artichokes and add to the cooker, with the stock, salt and pepper, making sure the cooker is no more than half full. Bring to high pressure and cook for 10 minutes.
3 Reduce pressure at room temperature. Sieve or liquidise the soup.
4 Add the milk and cream, reheat and serve sprinkled with chopped parsley.

To freeze:
5 Freeze after sieving or liquidising, but do not add the milk or cream. If liked, divide into two portions and freeze in suitable containers.
6 When serving, thaw and add half the milk to each portion; otherwise finish as before.

Leek and potato soup

cooking time: 5 minutes
pressure: high

you will need for 8 servings:

METRIC/IMPERIAL	
50 g/2 oz butter or	350 g/12 oz potatoes,
margarine	sliced
450 g/1 lb prepared leeks,	600 ml/1 pint chicken
sliced	stock
1 stick celery, sliced	salt and pepper

to serve:

300 ml/½ pint chicken	2 tablespoons chopped
150 ml/¼ pint single cream	parsley

1 Melt the butter or margarine in the cooker with the trivet removed. Put in the leeks and celery and cook gently without browning for 5 minutes.
2 Add the potatoes, stock, salt and pepper; bring to high pressure and cook for 5 minutes.
3 Reduce pressure at room temperature. Sieve or blend in a liquidiser.
4 Add the stock and re-heat gently. Serve the soup with the cream swirled on the top and sprinkled with parsley.

To freeze:
5 Freeze after sieving or liquidising. If liked, divide into two portions and freeze in suitable containers.
6 When serving, finish as before.

Spaghetti sauce

cooking time: 20 minutes
pressure: high

you will need for 8 servings:

METRIC/IMPERIAL
2 tablespoons corn oil
225 g/8 oz onions, finely chopped
100 g/4 oz carrots, chopped
1–2 cloves garlic, crushed
1 kg/2 lb fresh mince
300 ml/$\frac{1}{2}$ pint stock
1 (227-g/8-oz) can peeled tomatoes
1 (64-g/2$\frac{1}{4}$-oz) tomato purée
1 teaspoon salt
$\frac{1}{2}$ teaspoon pepper
1 teaspoon dried mixed herbs
2 bay leaves
100 g/4 oz mushrooms, chopped

1 Heat the oil in the cooker with the trivet removed, put in the onions and cook gently to lightly brown.
2 Add the carrots and garlic and cook for 5 minutes. Add the mince; stir round to brown all over.
3 Put in the remaining ingredients, making sure the cooker is no more than half full. Bring to high pressure and cook for 20 minutes.
4 Allow pressure to reduce at room temperature. Either serve immediately with spaghetti or freeze.

To freeze:
5 Allow to cool before freezing, line two separators with thick polythene freezer bags and divide the mince between the two. Seal and freeze in the separators.

To thaw:
6 Take one portion out of the polythene bag and put it in a solid separator; cover with foil.
7 Fill the cooker with 600 ml/1 pint water, stand the separator on the trivet, bring to high pressure and cook for 18 minutes.

Goulash with peppers

cooking time: 15 minutes
pressure: high

you will need for 6–8 servings:

METRIC/IMPERIAL
1 boned leg of lamb
2 tablespoons plain flour
1 tablespoon paprika
$\frac{1}{4}$ teaspoon chilli powder
3 tablespoons corn oil
2 sticks celery, sliced
1 large onion, sliced
225 g/8 oz green pepper, deseeded and chopped
1 (793-g/1 lb 12-oz) can peeled tomatoes
1 teaspoon sugar
bay leaf
salt and pepper
meat stock (can be made from the bones)

to serve:
150 ml/$\frac{1}{4}$ pint soured cream
150 ml/$\frac{1}{4}$ pint natural yogurt

1 Cut the meat into 1-cm/$\frac{1}{2}$-inch cubes, trimming off excess fat. Mix the flour, paprika and chilli powder together and use it to coat the meat.
2 Heat the oil in the cooker with the trivet removed, put in the meat and brown it all over. Using a slotted spoon, transfer it on to a plate.
3 Add the celery, onion and pepper to the pan, and cook gently until lightly browned.
4 Return the meat to the pan. Drain the tomatoes, and make up the juice to 300 ml/$\frac{1}{2}$ pint with meat stock.
5 Add the tomatoes with the sugar, stock and juice, bay leaf, salt and pepper. Bring to high pressure and cook for 15 minutes.
6 Reduce pressure at room temperature.

To serve:
7 Blend the soured cream and yogurt together and serve separately. Serve with boiled rice or noodles.

To freeze:
8 Allow to become cold and divide into two, place in suitable plastic containers, seal, label and freeze.

To thaw:
9 Place frozen stew in container of suitable size for the cooker and cover with foil. Pour 600 ml/1 pint water into the cooker, stand the dish on the trivet, bring to high pressure and cook for 4–5 minutes if thawed or 18 minutes if still frozen. Serve as before.

Veal mince

cooking time: 15 minutes
pressure: high

you will need for 8 servings:

METRIC/IMPERIAL
1 tablespoon oil
675 g/1$\frac{1}{2}$ lb veal mince
100 g/4 oz onion, grated
100 g/4 oz carrot, grated
100 g/4 oz mushrooms, grated
450 ml/$\frac{3}{4}$ pint veal stock
2 tablespoons tomato purée
1 clove garlic, crushed
$\frac{1}{2}$ teaspoon dried oregano
salt and pepper
1 tablespoon plain flour

1 Heat the oil in the cooker with the trivet removed. Stir in the mince and cook gently, stirring, to seal in the juices.
2 Add the remaining ingredients, except the flour, and mix well. Bring to high pressure and cook for 15 minutes.
3 Reduce pressure at room temperature. Blend the flour with a little water, add some hot stock, stir into the cooker, bring to the boil, stirring, and cook for 1 minute.
4 Serve half the quantity with rice or noodles or use to make lasagne. Freeze the rest, putting it into container; seal and label it.

To thaw:
5 Either thaw at room temperature or put it in a dish to fit the cooker, cover with foil and tie down.
6 Pour 600 ml/1 pint water into the cooker, place the dish on the trivet. Bring to high pressure for 18 minutes if frozen, or 3–4 minutes if thawed.
7 Reduce pressure at room temperature and serve as before.

Beef in red wine

cooking time: 20 minutes
pressure: high

you will need for 8 servings:

METRIC/IMPERIAL	
1·5 kg/3 lb shin of beef	bay leaf
1 tablespoon oil	225 g/8 oz button
225 g/8 oz onions, sliced	mushrooms, washed
into eighths	175 g/6 oz button onions,
450 ml/¾ pint beef stock,	peeled but whole
or water and 2 stock	175 g/6 oz carrots, sliced
cubes	pinch sugar
300 ml/½ pint red wine	
2 teaspoons tomato purée	*for beurre manie:*
2 cloves garlic, crushed	25 g/1 oz butter, softened
salt and pepper	25 g/1 oz flour

1 Trim the meat of sinew and fat, and cut into 2-cm/1-inch cubes.
2 Heat the oil in the cooker with the trivet removed, put in the meat and stir round until lightly browned.
3 Add the sliced onions, stock, wine, purée, garlic, salt, pepper and bay leaf. Bring to high pressure and cook for 15 minutes.
4 Reduce pressure with cold water. Stir in the mushrooms, onions, carrots and sugar. Return to high pressure and cook for 5 minutes.
5 Reduce pressure at room temperature. Blend the butter and flour together and add in pieces to the stew; stir round, heat gently to dissolve, bring just to the boil and cook for 1 minute to thicken.
6 Remove the bay leaf. Serve with noodles.

Variations:
a Add peeled canned chestnuts instead of the onions.
b Add a few pimento-stuffed olives.

Lamb casserole with rosemary

cooking time: 15 minutes
pressure: high
you will need for 6–8 servings:

METRIC/IMPERIAL	
1-kg/2-lb boned shoulder	salt and pepper
of lamb	2 sprigs of rosemary
2 tablespoons oil	1 green pepper, deseeded
1 large onion, chopped	and cut into large dice
1 clove garlic (optional)	225 g/8 oz courgettes,
1 (396-g/14-oz) can peeled	sliced and blanched for
tomatoes	2 minutes (optional)
150 ml/¼ pint red wine	2 teaspoons arrowroot

1 Cut the meat into cubes, removing some of the fat. Heat the oil in the cooker with the trivet removed, put in the meat and stir round.
2 Add the onion, garlic if used, tomatoes, wine, salt, pepper, rosemary and green pepper, making sure the cooker is no more than half full. Bring to high pressure and cook for 15 minutes.
3 Reduce pressure at room temperature. Add the courgettes and cook in the open cooker until just tender.
4 Blend the arrowroot with water, add some of the hot stock, return to the cooker and bring to the boil, stirring gently until the arrowroot thickens and clears.
5 Remove the rosemary before serving.

Cooking for one or two

A pressure cooker is ideal for cooking for one or two people, especially where equipment may be limited, as it can be used to prepare a complete meal.
Try these recipes which have all been tested and specially selected for convenience and economy.

Pork chops with orange

cooking time: 12 minutes
pressure: high

you will need for 2 servings:

METRIC/IMPERIAL	
2 teaspoons corn oil	2 tablespoons orange
2 pork chops	marmalade
1 onion	1 teaspoon wine vinegar
1 orange	salt and pepper

1 Heat the oil in the cooker with the trivet removed, put in the chops and cook to lightly brown each side.
2 Remove the chops and place each on a separate piece of foil large enough to enclose it. Add the onion to the cooker and cook for a few minutes to lightly brown.

Grate the orange rind. Stir in the marmalade, rind and vinegar, salt and pepper, heat to just melt the marmalade. Spoon over each chop.

Using a sharp knife, cut the pith from the orange and cut the orange into 4 slices. Place 2 slices on each chop. Fold over the foil to make a parcel.

Pour water into the cooker, place the trivet in the bottom and put the parcels on the trivet. Bring to high pressure and cook for 12 minutes.

Reduce pressure at room temperature. Serve with mashed potatoes and peas.

Chicken with lemon and rosemary

cooking time: 10 minutes
pressure: high

you will need for 2 servings:

METRIC/IMPERIAL
15 g/½ oz butter or margarine	3 tablespoons honey
2 chicken joints	salt and pepper
grated rind of I lemon and juice of ½ lemon	2 sprigs of rosemary

Melt the butter or margarine in the cooker with the trivet removed, fry the chicken quickly to brown all over. Remove the joints and place on a piece of foil. Put the rind and juice of lemon in the cooker with the honey, salt and pepper. Stir round and spoon over the chicken joints; put a sprig of rosemary on each. Fold over foil to make a parcel.

Pour 300 ml/½ pint water in the cooker. Place the foil parcel on the trivet, bring to high pressure and cook for 10 minutes.

Reduce pressure at room temperature. Lift the joints from the foil and pour the juices over each.

Hint:
If liked, accompanying vegetables could be added in the separator and placed in the cooker halfway through the cooking time. See vegetable cooking chart page 64 for cooking times.

Lamb's tongues with parsley sauce

cooking time: 15 minutes
pressure: high

you will need for 2 servings:

METRIC/IMPERIAL
4 lamb's tongues	I tablespoon chopped parsley
300 ml/½ pint water	½ teaspoon made English mustard
I carrot, peeled	
I onion, peeled	salt and pepper
bay leaf	
I tablespoon cornflour	

1 Wash and trim away the roots (or bone) from the tongues.
2 Place in the cooker with the trivet removed with the water, whole carrot and onion and bay leaf. Bring to high pressure and cook for 15 minutes.
3 Reduce pressure at room temperature. Transfer the tongues to a plate. When cool enough to handle, peel off the skin.
4 Remove and chop the onion and carrot. Blend the cornflour with a little water, add some hot stock and return to the cooker with the vegetables, parsley, mustard, salt and pepper.
5 Bring slowly to the boil, stirring, and cook for 1 minute until sauce thickens and clears.
6 Slice each tongue lengthways into 3 or 4 and return slices to the sauce, heat through. Serve with mashed potatoes.

● **Hint:**
The cooker may be opened 5 minutes before the end of cooking time and prepared vegetables placed in the separators. Return to pressure and cook for remaining cooking time.

Bacon with apple and sage sauce

cooking time: 8 minutes
pressure: high

you will need for I serving:

METRIC/IMPERIAL
I bacon chop	grated rind and juice of ½ lemon
2 medium carrots, peeled	
I medium potato, peeled	large pinch dried sage
I small cooking apple, peeled, cored and sliced	1–2 teaspoons castor sugar
	salt and pepper

1 Put bacon chop in base of open cooker and heat gently to extract a little fat and lightly brown the chop on both sides. Lift the chop from the pan.
2 Put 300 ml/½ pint water in the cooker, replace trivet and place the chop on top and to one side with the carrots and potato cut into quarters.
3 Put apple, lemon rind and juice, sage and sugar in a small bowl beside the chop and cover top with a double thickness of greaseproof paper; tie down. Bring to high pressure and cook for 8 minutes.
4 Reduce pressure at room temperature. Lift out the bowl of apple and mix in salt and pepper to taste and a small knob of butter, adding more sugar if necessary. Serve with the chop.

● **Hint:**
Remember other vegetables can also be added to the pan, depending on the size of the cooker. They should be of an even size.

Rabbit in mustard sauce

cooking time: 20 minutes
pressure: high

you will need for 2 servings:

METRIC/IMPERIAL
2 rashers streaky bacon, trimmed and chopped
2–4 rabbit joints
8–12 button onions
3 small carrots
300 ml/½ pint stock
1 tablespoon French mustard
1 teaspoon lemon juice
salt and pepper
3–4 tablespoons soured cream
1 tablespoon cornflour

1 Put bacon in the cooker with the trivet removed and cook gently to extract the fat. Add joints and fry until brown on all sides.
2 Add onions, carrots, stock, mustard and lemon juice. Season to taste. Bring to high pressure and cook for 20 minutes.
3 Reduce pressure with cold water. Blend soured cream with the cornflour and mix into pan. Return cooker to heat and bring to the boil, stirring.

Variations:

a This recipe could also be used for chicken joints. Cook for 7 minutes.
b Try 225 g/8 oz veal and ham, cubed and cooked for 15 minutes, instead of the rabbit.

Kidney in mushroom yogurt sauce

cooking time: 5 minutes
pressure: high

you will need for I serving:

METRIC/IMPERIAL
15 g/½ oz butter
1 pig's kidney, prepared and sliced
1 small onion, finely chopped
50 g/2 oz mushrooms, sliced
1 tablespoon tomato ketchup
150 ml/¼ pint stock
salt and pepper
2 medium potatoes, peeled and halved
2 tablespoons yogurt
1 egg yolk

1 Melt butter in the cooker with the trivet removed, put in the kidney and onion and cook, stirring, until lightly brown.
2 Mix in the mushrooms and cook for 1 minute. Stir in tomato ketchup, stock and seasoning.
3 Place trivet over the kidney and put the potatoes on top. Bring to high pressure and cook for 5 minutes.
4 Reduce pressure with cold water. Put potatoes on a hot dish. Remove trivet and stir the yogurt and egg yolk into the stock to thicken.

Variations:

a Lamb's liver could be used instead of kidney.
b Cider and stock in equal proportions could be used instead of all stock.
c 1 teaspoon of capers could be added.

Beef and peanut stew

cooking time: 20 minutes
pressure: high

you will need for 2 servings:

METRIC/IMPERIAL
1 tablespoon oil
1 medium onion, chopped
225 g/8 oz stewing beef, trimmed and cut into 2·5-cm/1-inch cubes
1 carrot, chopped
225 g/8 oz potatoes
1 stick celery, sliced (optional)
2 tablespoons tomato purée or ketchup
300 ml/½ pint beef stock
bay leaf
25–50 g/1–2 oz salted peanuts
salt and pepper
1 tablespoon cornflour

1 Heat oil in the cooker with the trivet removed, put in the onion and beef and sauté until lightly browned.
2 Add carrot, potatoes, celery (if using), purée or ketchup, stock, bay leaf, peanuts and seasoning. Bring to high pressure and cook for 20 minutes.
3 Reduce pressure with cold water. Return open cooker to stove and thicken the gravy with cornflour blended with a little water.

Variations:

a Red wine may be used instead of stock.
b Any root vegetables could be added.

Braised celery with black pudding

cooking time: 4 minutes
pressure: high

you will need for 2 servings:

METRIC/IMPERIAL
25 g/1 oz butter
1 clove garlic, crushed
1 small head celery, trimmed and cut into quarters
1 (227-g/8-oz) can tomatoes
150 ml/¼ pint stock
1 tablespoon cornflour
175–225 g/6–8 oz black pudding, sliced
salt and pepper

1 Heat butter in the cooker with the trivet removed and sauté the garlic and celery for 1–2 minutes.
2 Pour in the tomatoes and their juice, stock and seasoning. Bring to high pressure and cook for 4 minutes.
3 Reduce pressure with cold water. Return cooker to the heat and thicken sauce with the cornflour blended with a little water.
4 Add the pudding and heat through well before serving.

Spiced lamb and lentil stew

cooking time: 15 minutes
pressure: high

you will need for 2 servings:

METRIC/IMPERIAL

1 medium onion, sliced	300 ml/½ pint stock
1 medium carrot, sliced	juice of ½ lemon
125–175 g/4–6 oz lamb fillet, cut into portions	salt and pepper
100 g/4 oz lentils	25 g/1 oz sultanas
2 teaspoons curry powder	1 tablespoon redcurrant jelly
large pinch chilli powder or seasoning	

1 Put the onion, carrot, lamb, lentils, curry and chilli powder in the cooker with the trivet removed. Add stock, lemon juice and seasoning to taste; bring to the boil and stir.
2 Bring to high pressure and cook for 15 minutes. Reduce pressure with cold water.
3 Return the cooker to the heat and stir in the sultanas and redcurrant jelly. Cook for 2 minutes or until well blended.

Lamb with orange sauce

cooking time: 10 minutes
pressure: high

you will need for 2 servings:

METRIC/IMPERIAL

2 lamb chump chops	1 small onion, grated
grated rind and juice of 1 orange	milk
1 slice white bread, trimmed and cubed	salt and pepper
	pinch mixed herbs
	1 tablespoon oil

1 Make a cut from the fat side of the chops to the bone to make a large pocket to take the stuffing.
2 Mix the orange rind with the bread and half the onion. Moisten the mixture with milk and beat well with a fork until fairly smooth. Add seasoning and mixed herbs. Divide stuffing between the chops and secure the edge with a cocktail stick.
3 Heat the oil in the open cooker with the trivet removed, put in the chops and brown on both sides. Remove them from the pan.
4 Add remaining onion to the pan and cook for 1 minute. Pour in orange juice made up to 150 ml/¼ pint with water.
5 Return the trivet to the cooker and arrange the chops on top. Bring to high pressure and cook for 6 minutes. Reduce the pressure with cold water.
6 Meanwhile, place vegetables in the separators and put them in the cooker. Bring to high pressure and cook for 4 minutes.
7 Reduce the pressure with cold water. Dish up the vegetables and chops. Blend cornflour to a smooth paste, stir into the cooker and cook until the sauce is thickened. Pour over the chops and serve.

● **Hint:**
If cooking for one, cook both chops with sauce. The other can be served cold the next day.

Lamb and barley stew

cooking time: 20 minutes
pressure: high

you will need for 2 servings:

METRIC/IMPERIAL

350 g/12 oz scrag end of lamb, chopped into portions	225 g/8 oz potatoes, peeled and sliced
1 large onion, sliced	300 ml/½ pint stock or water
1 large carrot, sliced	salt and pepper
25 g/1 oz pearl barley	

1 Arrange meat in the base of the open cooker with the trivet removed.
2 Mix stock with salt and pepper and pour into the cooker; bring to the boil.
3 Stir in the onion, carrot and pearl barley; place the potatoes neatly over the top. Bring to high pressure and cook for 20 minutes. Reduce pressure with cold water.

Variations:
a Use leeks to replace onions.
b Use long-grain rice to replace barley.

Lamb with haricot beans

cooking time: 20 minutes
pressure: high

you will need for 2 servings:

METRIC/IMPERIAL

100 g/4 oz haricot beans	275 g/8 oz carrots, sliced
1 tablespoon oil	300 ml/½ pint stock
350 g/12 oz middle neck of lamb, jointed	good pinch rosemary or mixed herbs
1 onion, sliced	salt and pepper

1 Soak the dried beans in boiling water for at least 10 minutes.
2 Heat oil in the open cooker with the trivet removed and sauté the lamb until brown on both sides. Add onion and carrots and cook gently for a further 3–4 minutes.
3 Pour in the stock, rosemary or herbs and salt and pepper to taste. Bring to high pressure and cook for 20 minutes.
4 Reduce pressure at room temperature.

Variations:
a Substitute sliced leeks for onion.
b Use wine in place of the stock.

Pork and cabbage hot pot

cooking time: 20 minutes
pressure: high

you will need for 2 servings:

METRIC/IMPERIAL
1 tablespoon oil	¼ small firm white cabbage
350 g/12 oz lean pork, cut into cubes	300 ml/½ pint dry cider
1 small onion, sliced	½ teaspoon caraway seeds
1 small carrot, sliced	salt and pepper
1 dessert apple, peeled, cored and sliced	1 tablespoon cornflour

1 Heat oil in the open cooker with the trivet removed, put in the pork and cook until lightly brown. Add onion and cook for 3–4 minutes.
2 Add carrot, apple, cabbage, cider and caraway seeds and season with salt and pepper. Bring to high pressure and cook for 15 minutes.
3 Reduce pressure with cold water. Add the cabbage and return to high pressure and cook for a further 5 minutes.
4 Blend cornflour to a smooth paste with a little extra cider or water.
5 Remove cabbage, stir cornflour into pan and cook for 2 minutes until mixture thickens.

Variations:

a Omit onion and add chopped spring onions with the cider.
b Substitute for the cider grated rind and juice of 1 lemon made up to 300 ml/½ pint with stock.

Braised beef with butter beans

cooking time: 20 minutes
pressure: high

you will need for 2 servings:

METRIC/IMPERIAL
100 g/4 oz butter beans	300 ml/½ pint beef stock
1 tablespoon oil	2 tablespoons tomato purée
225 g/8 oz braising beef	pinch mixed herbs
1 onion, chopped	salt and pepper
2 carrots, sliced	
1 medium turnip, chopped	

1 Soak the beans in boiling water for at least 10 minutes.
2 Heat oil in the open cooker with the trivet removed and sauté the beef and onions until lightly brown.
3 Add drained beans, carrot, turnip, stock, herbs and tomato purée and mix well. Add seasoning.
4 Bring to high pressure and cook for 20 minutes. Reduce the pressure with cold water.

Beef and bean stew

cooking time: 15 minutes
pressure: high

you will need for 2 servings:

METRIC/IMPERIAL
100 g/4 oz red kidney beans	1 parsnip or small turnip
1 tablespoon oil	1 (227-g/8-oz) can tomatoes
1 medium onion, chopped	300 ml/½ pint stock
225 g/8 oz stewing beef, cut in 2·5-cm/1-inch cubes	bay leaf
1 carrot, sliced	salt and pepper
	dash of Tabasco sauce

1 Soak the beans in boiling water for at least 10 minutes, then drain.
2 Heat the oil in the open cooker with the trivet removed, put in the onion and beef and sauté until lightly brown on all sides.
3 Add the drained beans, carrot, parsnip or turnip, tomatoes and their juice, stock, bay leaf, salt, pepper and Tabasco sauce. Bring to high pressure and cook for 15 minutes.
4 Reduce pressure with cold water.

Paprika mince with noodles

cooking time: 15 minutes
pressure: high

you will need for 1 serving:

METRIC/IMPERIAL
1 tablespoon oil	250 ml/½ pint stock
1 small onion, chopped	salt and pepper
100 g/4 oz beef mince	25 g/1 oz noodles
2 teaspoons paprika	
2 tablespoons dried green and red peppers	

1 Heat the oil in the cooker with the trivet removed, put in the onion and sauté until lightly brown.
2 Add mince and paprika and cook for a further few minutes. Add dried peppers, stock and seasoning to taste.
3 Bring to high pressure and cook for 11 minutes. Reduce pressure with cold water.
4 Mix noodles into the meat. Bring to high pressure again and cook for 4 minutes.

Variations:

a Use red or white wine to replace some stock.
b Minced lamb, pork or veal can be used instead of beef.
c Potatoes or rice can replace the noodles.

Liver and bacon stew

cooking time: 15 minutes
pressure: high

you will need for 1 serving:

METRIC/IMPERIAL

100 g/5 oz ox liver	200 ml/7 fl oz beef stock
1 teaspoon oil	or water
1–2 rashers streaky bacon,	2 small carrots, cut in
trimmed and chopped	quarters
1 small onion, chopped	2 small potatoes, cut in
1 tablespoon flour	quarters
salt and pepper	pinch sugar

1 Cut the liver into cubes and soak in a little milk for 10 minutes.
2 Heat the oil in the open cooker with the trivet removed, add the bacon and cook gently until the fat starts to run from the bacon, then add the onion and cook for 5 minutes.
3 Drain the liver, then toss it in the flour seasoned with a little salt and pepper. Add the liver to the cooker and sauté, stirring, until lightly brown.
4 Add stock or water, bring to high pressure and cook for 11 minutes. Reduce pressure with cold water.
5 Meanwhile, sprinkle the vegetables with a little seasoning and arrange either on the trivet or in a separator. Put them in the cooker, return it to high pressure and cook for 4 minutes.
6 Reduce pressure with cold water. Turn the vegetables out on to a serving dish. Thicken the sauce with the remaining flour blended smoothly with water and cook for 2–3 minutes.
7 Check seasoning, add sugar and serve at once.

Variations:

a Add a small pinch of dried mixed herbs.
b Stir in 2 teaspoons tomato ketchup at the end.

Vegetables

When cooking vegetables in the pressure cooker one must be selective and allow for a certain amount of trial and error. Age and freshness determine the length of cooking time required and this also depends on the size of the vegetable pieces which have been prepared.

I have included a number of vegetable dishes which normally take a long time to cook in order to show how versatile vegetables can be.

Vegetable cooking chart

The times given vary according to the size of the vegetables and their age.

Vegetable preparation	Cooking time (high pressure)	Blanching time for freezing (medium pressure)	Serving suggestion
Asparagus Wash, trim and tie in bundles each containing 4–6 spears. Place on trivet.	2–4 minutes	Just bring to pressure	With melted butter, hollandaise or mousseline sauce.
Broad beans Pod and place in separator.	4–5 minutes	1 minute	With parsley sauce.
Beetroot (see note) Cut off tops, leaving 2·5 cm/ 1 inch of stem. Peel when cooked.	10 minutes (small) 15–20 minutes (medium) 25–30 minutes (large)	7 minutes (sliced)	Hot with béchamel sauce or soured cream: cold with vinegar.
Broccoli Trim and divide into spears. Place in separator.	3–4 minutes	1 minute	With melted butter and a sprinkling of nutmeg or ground black pepper.
Brussels sprouts Trim and cut a cross in the base of each. Place in separator.	3–4 minutes	1 minute	With cooked chestnuts, melted butter or a sprinkling of grated nutmeg.
Cabbage Trim, discard stalk and shred. Place in separator.	3 minutes	Just bring to pressure	With melted butter, or a few caraway seeds.
Carrots Peel, slice, or cut into sticks. Young ones may be left whole. Place in separator, or on the trivet.	3–4 minutes	2 minutes	With melted butter, black pepper and chopped parsley.
Cauliflower Trim and divide into sprigs. Place on the trivet.	3–4 minutes 5–8 minutes (whole)	1 minute	With béchamel or cheese sauce.

Celery Trim and cut into 5-cm/2-inch lengths. Place in separator, or on trivet.	3–4 minutes	2 minutes	With béchamel sauce.
Celeriac Peel and cube, or cut into 2·5-cm/1-inch sticks. Cover with cold water until ready to place in separator.	3 minutes	1 minute	With parsley or cheese sauce.
Chicory Discard any loose outer leaves. Place whole on trivet, dot with butter and sprinkle with lemon juice.	3–6 minutes	Not suitable for freezing	With béchamel or cheese sauce.
Corn-on-the-cob Remove leaves and silks. Place whole on trivet.	3 minutes (small) 5 minutes (large)	2 minutes 3 minutes	With ground black pepper and melted butter.
Courgettes Slice. Place in separator.	3 minutes	Just bring to pressure	With melted butter, black pepper and chopped chives.
Fennel Trim, discard leafy tops and halve. Place on trivet.	3–6 minutes	1 minute	With cheese sauce.
French beans Top, tail and place on trivet.	3 minutes	Just bring to pressure	With melted butter, or cold in a salad.
Globe artichokes Remove outer leaves. Place on trivet.	6 minutes (small) 10 minutes (large)	3 minutes (small) 5 minutes (large)	With melted butter, or French dressing.
Jerusalem artichokes Peel. Place on trivet.	4–5 minutes	Freeze cooked as a purée with lemon juice added. Use for soup.	With melted butter and black pepper.
Kohl-rabi Discard outer leaves, peel and cut into 5-mm/¼-inch slices. Place in separator.	4 minutes		With cheese or hollandaise sauce.
Leeks Trim and slice. Wash well. Place in separator.	2–3 minutes	1 minute	With béchamel or cheese sauce.
Marrow Skin, slice thickly and discard seeds. Place on trivet.	4 minutes	2 minutes	With béchamel or cheese sauce.

Vegetable preparation	Cooking time (high pressure)	Blanching time for freezing (medium pressure)	Serving suggestion
Onions Peel and slice. Place in separator.	4 minutes	Not really worth freezing	With béchamel or cheese sauce.
Peel, leave whole and place on trivet.	6–8 minutes		
Parsnips Peel and cube. Place in separator or on trivet.	3–4 minutes	1 minute	With butter and black pepper.
Peas Shell. Place in separator with a sprig of mint.	3–4 minutes	1 minute	With melted butter.
Potatoes (new) Scrape and leave whole. Place in separator or on trivet.	4–5 minutes	2 minutes	With melted butter and chopped parsley or chives.
Potatoes (old) Peel and quarter. Place in separator or on trivet.	3–4 minutes	Not really worth freezing	Creamed with butter and hot milk: with a knob of butter and chopped parsley.
Runner beans String and slice.	4 minutes	To pressure only	With a knob of butter.
Swedes Peel and cube. Place in separator.	4 minutes	1 minute	Mashed with butter and seasoned with black pepper.
Turnips Peel and slice. Place in separator.	3–4 minutes	2 minutes	Mashed with butter.
Young, whole, place on trivet or in separator.	3–4 minutes	2 minutes	With melted butter and black pepper.

Note
When pressure cooking beetroots, as the cooking time is longer, a greater amount of water must be put in the cooker before it is brought to pressure.

For small beetroots allow 600 ml/1 pint water.
For medium beetroots allow 1½ pints/900 ml water.
For large beetroots allow generous litre/2 pints water.

Scalloped potatoes

cooking time: 15 minutes
pressure: high
you will need for 4 servings:

METRIC/IMPERIAL
450 g/1 lb potatoes
25 g/1 oz butter
1 onion, thinly sliced
salt and pepper
150 ml/¼ pint milk

1 Peel and thinly slice the potatoes. Lightly butter a 1-litre/1¾-pint soufflé dish.
2 Arrange in alternate layers the potatoes, onion, a few flakes of butter, salt and pepper, finishing with a layer of potato.
3 Pour over it the milk, cover with 2 layers of grease-proof paper and tie round with string.
4 Keeping the trivet in the cooker, pour in 300 ml/½ pint water; place the dish on the trivet, bring to high pressure, and cook for 15 minutes.
5 Reduce heat at room temperature, remove grease-proof paper and serve.

Sweet and sour cabbage

cooking time: 3 minutes
pressure: high

you will need for 4–6 servings:

METRIC/IMPERIAL
1 kg/2 lb red or white
  firm cabbage
50 g/2 oz butter
1 large onion, sliced
350 g/12 oz cooking
  apples, sliced
1 tablespoon red or white
  wine vinegar
salt and pepper
150 ml/¼ pint chicken
2 tablespoons demerara
  sugar
25 g/1 oz sultanas

Wash and shred the cabbage fairly finely, discarding any thick stalks.
Melt the butter in the cooker with the trivet removed, add the onion and cabbage and toss around in the butter.
Add the remaining ingredients. Bring to high pressure and cook for 3 minutes.
Reduce pressure at room temperature. Serve with pork, goose or duck.

Cauliflower cheese

cooking time: 3–4 minutes (see method)
pressure: high

you will need for 3–4 servings:

METRIC/IMPERIAL
1 medium cauliflower
300 ml/½ pint water
salt and pepper
25 g/1 oz butter or
  margarine
25 g/1 oz plain flour
150 ml/¼ pint milk
75 g/3 oz strong Cheddar
  cheese, grated

1 Remove the tougher outside leaves of the cauliflower and leave the head whole. Using a potato peeler, scoop out as much of the thick stem as possible and wash the cauliflower.
2 Place the cauliflower in the cooker with the trivet removed, add the water, salt and pepper. Bring to high pressure and cook for 3–4 minutes, depending on size.
3 Reduce pressure with cold water, lift out the cauliflower carefully and drain before placing in a flame-proof dish. Reserve 150 ml/¼ pint of the cauliflower stock.
4 Melt the butter or margarine in a saucepan, add the flour and gradually stir in the stock and milk. Bring to the boil, stirring, and cook for 2 minutes until thickened.
5 Stir in most of the cheese, add salt and pepper, pour the sauce over the cauliflower and sprinkle with the remaining cheese.
6 Place under a preheated grill to lightly brown.

Variations:

a Try 100 g/4 oz crumbled Danish blue cheese instead of Cheddar cheese.
b Top the cauliflower with fried crispy bacon, crumbled, and sprinkle with chopped parsley.
c For added savoury flavour, add 1 teaspoon vegetable extract to the melting fat when making the sauce.
d Grated onion and a small clove of crushed garlic complement the cheese sauce.

Red cabbage braise

cooking time: 5 minutes
pressure: high

you will need for 6–8 servings:

METRIC/IMPERIAL
50 g/2 oz butter
50 g/2 oz demerara sugar
4 tablespoons water
4 tablespoons white
  vinegar
1 kg/2 lb red cabbage,
  shredded
salt and pepper

1 Melt the butter in the cooker with the trivet removed, add the sugar, water and vinegar and stir round over a low heat to dissolve.
2 Put in the cabbage and stir around, making sure the cooker is no more than half full. Bring to high pressure and cook for 5 minutes.
3 Reduce pressure with cold water. Stir round before serving as a vegetable.

Variations:

a Sliced apple and a few sultanas could be added.
b Instead of water and vinegar, add cider.
c A little redcurrant jelly stirred in at the end gives a richness to the cabbage.

Leeks niçoise

cooking time: 4 minutes
pressure: high

you will need for 4 servings:

METRIC/IMPERIAL
8 medium white leeks
4 tablespoons olive oil
1 clove garlic, crushed

to garnish:
1 tablespoon chopped
  parsley

salt and pepper
225 g/8 oz tomatoes,
  peeled and sliced

1 Trim the leeks and wash very thoroughly to remove any grit.
2 Put the oil in the cooker with the trivet removed, add the garlic, salt and pepper.
3 Place the leeks side by side in the base of the cooker. Arrange the sliced tomatoes on top of the leeks. Bring to high pressure and cook for 4 minutes.
4 Reduce pressure with cold water. Serve sprinkled with chopped parsley.

Variations:

a If liked, add a few stuffed olives to the leeks.
b ¼ teaspoon dried oregano or marjoram would be a tasty addition.

Curried vegetable stew

cooking time: 3 minutes
pressure: high

you will need for 4 servings:

METRIC/IMPERIAL
2 tablespoons oil
225 g/8 oz onions
2 tablespoons curry
  powder
40 g/1½ oz plain flour
1 clove garlic, crushed
1 tablespoon vegetable
  extract
600 ml/1 pint water
1 tablespoon tomato purée

1 teaspoon sugar
1 small cauliflower,
  trimmed and sprigged
225 g/8 oz carrots, sliced
225 g/8 oz courgettes, cut
  in 1-cm/½-inch slices
100 g/4 oz button
  mushrooms
3 tomatoes, peeled and
  quartered

1 Heat the oil in the cooker with the trivet removed, put in the onions and cook for 5 minutes. Stir in the curry powder.
2 Stir in the flour, garlic, vegetable extract and gradually stir in the water. Bring to the boil, stirring, and cook for 2 minutes until thickened.
3 Add the remaining ingredients. Bring to high pressure and cook for 3 minutes.
4 Reduce pressure with cold water. Serve with banana, poppadoms, peanuts, chutney and redcurrant jelly.

Variation:

Use parsnip instead of the courgettes.

● **Hint:**
The vegetables must be slightly crisp to give the dish texture.

Braised fennel

cooking time: 5 minutes
pressure: high

you will need for 4 servings:

METRIC/IMPERIAL
1 teaspoon oil
4 rashers streaky bacon,
  rind removed and cut
  into small pieces
1 small onion, finely
  chopped

575 g/1¼ lb fennel
150 ml/¼ pint water
¼ teaspoon dried thyme
salt and freshly ground
  pepper

1 Heat the oil in the cooker with the trivet removed, add the bacon and onion, cook gently to extract the fat from the bacon for a few minutes.
2 Meanwhile, trim the ends off the fennel and cut each bulb in half or quarters depending on the size.
3 Add to the cooker with the remaining ingredients. Bring to high pressure and cook for 5 minutes.
4 Reduce pressure with cold water. Lift out the fennel with the onion and bacon pieces on to a heated serving dish. Keep hot.
5 If liked, reduce the liquor and pour it over the fennel.

Spinach and cheese pudding

cooking time: 20 minutes
pressure: high

you will need for 4 servings:

METRIC/IMPERIAL
150 ml/¼ pint milk
25 g/1 oz butter
bay leaf
50 g/2 oz fresh bread-
  crumbs
1 (227-g/8-oz) packet
  frozen spinach, thawed

3 eggs, separated
salt and pepper
little grated nutmeg
50 g/2 oz cheese, grated
600 ml/1 pint boiling
  water

1 Heat the milk, butter and bay leaf in a pan to just below boiling point, then remove from the heat.
3 Discard the bay leaf and pour the milk over the breadcrumbs. Leave to stand for 30 minutes.
4 Mix in the spinach, egg yolks, seasonings and cheese. Whisk the egg whites until stiff then fold into the spinach mixture.
5 Pour the mixture into a greased 1-litre/2-pint oven-proof bowl and cover with a double layer of greased greaseproof paper secured with string.
6 Pour the boiling water into the cooker and stand the bowl on the trivet. Bring to high pressure and cook for 20 minutes.
7 Allow the pressure to reduce at room temperature. Lift out the pudding, take off the papers and serve at once.

● **Hint:**
A green or winter salad is a good accompaniment to this spinach pudding.

Savoury stuffed onions

cooking time: 8 minutes
pressure: high

you will need for 4 servings:

METRIC/IMPERIAL

4 large onions	50 g/2 oz fresh bread-
300 ml/½ pint water	crumbs
25 g/1 oz butter	1 egg
100 g/4 oz bacon, chopped	2 tablespoons cream
salt and pepper	50 g/2 oz cheese, grated
pinch dry mustard	

1 Peel the onions, but leave whole. Put the water and trivet in the bottom of the cooker and place the onions on the trivet. Bring to high pressure and cook for 8 minutes.
2 Meanwhile, heat the butter in a pan and add the chopped bacon. Cook for 2–3 minutes, then stir in the seasonings and breadcrumbs and heat through.
3 Lightly beat the egg and cream together and mix into the bacon mixture. Leave on a low heat.
4 Reduce the pressure with cold water. Take out the onions, slice off the tops and remove the centres, leaving a shell 1–2·5 cm/½–1 inch thick. Chop the centres and tops and mix into the filling.
5 Place the onion shells in the grill pan with the rack removed and spoon in the filling. Sprinkle the tops with grated cheese and brown under a moderate grill.
6 If liked, serve with tomato sauce.

Variations:
a Use ham instead of bacon.
b Try mushrooms instead of bacon.
c Chopped hazel or peanuts could be substituted for the bacon.

Vegetarian dishes

Although not a vegetarian myself, I have enjoyed creating these interesting and nutritious dishes. I find that the variation of texture, which is important in vegetarian cooking, helps to make these dishes really delicious.

The best advantage of using a pressure cooker is that I have been able to reduce greatly the soaking time of such items as dried beans, which enables these long-soak and long-cook ingredients to be used more often. I find I am easily put off by a recipe which indicates an overnight soak for the dried ingredients.

Pulse foods, which are used in many of these recipes, are an economical and valuable source of protein, vitamins and minerals which makes them a cheap substitute for meat.

I hope that many of these recipes will appeal to vegetarians as well as to those of us who are looking for more economical family meals.

Rice

cooking time: 5 minutes
pressure: high

you will need for 4 servings:

METRIC/IMPERIAL
½ litre/I pint water or stock   250 g/9 oz long-grain rice
    salt and pepper

1 Put the water or stock in the cooker with the trivet removed and bring to the boil. Stir in the rice.
2 Bring to high pressure and cook for 5 minutes.
3 Reduce pressure with water, stir round and season.

Variations:

a Fry a little onion in oil, add stock and stir in the rice.
b A few herbs added, or a herb stock cube gives an interesting flavour and could be the base of a nice dish.
c Lemon rind and chopped parsley makes a pleasant change.
d A pinch of turmeric gives a spicy yellow rice. Saffron is nice to use but expensive, and has nearly the same result as turmeric.

● **Hint:**
It is important to stir the rice to help the grains to separate.

Curried rice

cooking time: 8 minutes
pressure: high

you will need for 4 servings:

METRIC/IMPERIAL
3 tablespoons oil   600 ml/I pint stock
I large onion, sliced   50 g/2 oz raisins
100 g/4 oz button   50 g/2 oz stuffed olives
    mushrooms   25 g/I oz salted peanuts
225 g/8 oz long-grain rice   salt and pepper
I tablespoon curry powder
I small eating apple, chopped

1 Heat the oil in the open cooker with the trivet removed, fry the onion until it begins to brown. Add the mushrooms, rice and curry powder, stir round and cook for 1 minute.
2 Add the apple and stock, bring to the boil in the open cooker and stir. Bring to high pressure and cook for 8 minutes.
3 Reduce pressure with cold water. Stir in the remaining ingredients and just heat them. Serve with chutney and a green salad.

Variation:
Black olives could be used instead of stuffed olives, and the rice could be sprinkled with paprika.

Lentil and vegetable curry

cooking time: 20 minutes
pressure: high

you will need for 3–4 servings:

METRIC/IMPERIAL
2 tablespoons pure corn oil   3 tomatoes, peeled and chopped
I large onion, chopped   2 teaspoons vegetable extract
I cooking apple, peeled, cored and diced   225 g/8 oz lentils
2–3 teaspoons curry powder   600 ml/I pint water
4 carrots, thickly sliced   salt and pepper

1 Heat the corn oil in the cooker with the trivet removed and sauté the onion, apple and curry powder together for 4 minutes.
2 Add all the remaining ingredients and mix well. Making sure the cooker is no more than half full, bring to high pressure over a low heat and cook for 20 minutes.
3 Serve with boiled rice, accompanied by sliced banana, peanuts and redcurrant jelly.

Savoury bread and butter pudding

cooking time: 10 minutes
pressure: high

you will need for 4 servings:

METRIC/IMPERIAL

75 g/3 oz butter or margarine	100 g/4 oz Cheddar cheese, grated
1 large onion, chopped	3 large eggs
1 tablespoon Marmite	salt and pepper
6 slices of bread, about 5 mm/¼ inch thick	600 ml/1 pint milk

1 Melt 15 g/½ oz of the butter in a small saucepan. Add the onion and fry gently for 5 minutes to soften.

2 Spread the bread with the remaining butter and a thin layer of Marmite.

3 Using a 1-litre/2-pint soufflé dish, place a layer of bread in the base and sprinkle over it some of the onion and cheese. Continue with these layers, ending with a layer of bread and a sprinkling of cheese.

4 Break the eggs in a bowl, add salt and pepper and beat with a fork. Heat the milk a little until lukewarm and pour on to the eggs. Strain the mixture over the bread and allow to stand for 4 minutes.

5 Cover the dish with double greaseproof paper and tie down. Put 300 ml/½ pint water in the cooker, arrange a foil sling under the dish to assist lifting, and place it on the trivet.

6 Bring to high pressure and cook for 10 minutes. Allow pressure to reduce at room temperature.

Variations:

Add ½ teaspoon dried mixed herbs to the custard.
Instead of Marmite, sauté 100 g/4 oz chopped bacon with the onion.
For a crisp top add a little extra cheese and put under a hot grill to melt.

Leek and bean crumble

cooking time: 12 minutes
pressure: high

you will need for 4-6 servings:

METRIC/IMPERIAL

350 g/12 oz mung beans	2 tablespoons flour
450 g/1 lb leeks, washed thoroughly	200 ml/7 fl oz milk
50 g/2 oz margarine	1 teaspoon dried thyme
	salt and pepper

for crumble:

150 g/5 oz wholemeal flour	50 g/2 oz strong Cheddar cheese, grated
75 g/3 oz margarine	

Wash the beans very thoroughly. Put them in the cooker with the trivet removed and add 300 ml/½ pint

water. Bring to high pressure and cook for 9 minutes.

2 Reduce pressure with cold water. Slice the leeks coarsely and add to the cooker. Return to high pressure and cook for 3 minutes.

3 Reduce pressure with cold water. Stir in the margarine until melted, sprinkle in the flour and mix carefully. Gradually stir in the milk over a low heat.

4 Stir in thyme, salt and pepper and cook for 1 minute. Turn into a shallow ovenproof dish.

5 Rub together margarine and flour, add the grated cheese, salt and pepper. Sprinkle the mixture over the vegetables.

6 Cook in a moderate oven 350°F, 180°C, Gas Mark 4 for 20 minutes.

7 Serve with green salad or carrots.

Nut loaf

cooking time: 32 minutes
pressure: high

you will need for 4 servings:

METRIC/IMPERIAL

175 g/6 oz mung beans	salt and pepper
450 ml/¾ pint water	175 g/6 oz hazelnuts, finely grated
75 g/3 oz butter	
225 g/8 oz onions, finely chopped	1 large egg
	little melted butter
1 clove garlic, crushed	1 tablespoon wholemeal flour
½ teaspoon basil	
1 tablespoon vegetable extract	

1 Put the beans in the cooker with the trivet removed, cover with boiling water and leave for 5 minutes.

2 Bring to high pressure and cook for 12 minutes. Reduce with cold water and drain the beans.

3 Melt the butter, put in the onions and sauté carefully. Add the garlic, basil, vegetable extract, salt and pepper; stir carefully until onions are cooked. Add beans and nuts to vegetable mixture and stir well. Beat the egg and add it to the mixture.

4 Thoroughly grease a 0·5-kg/1-lb loaf tin, base-line and brush with butter. Dust with the flour, add the mixture and press firmly into shape. Cover with a double layer of foil and seal under the rim.

5 Put 450 ml/¾ pint water in the cooker and place the loaf tin on the trivet. Bring to high pressure and cook for 20 minutes.

6 Reduce pressure with cold water. Turn out and serve with a tomato sauce.

Variations:

a Add 100 g/4 oz chopped mushrooms to the onions and use 2 standard eggs instead of 1 large.

b Mix 1 tablespoon tomato purée, 2 tablespoons soured cream together and spread over the top of the cooked loaf before serving. If liked, sprinkle with chopped chives or parsley.

Savoury soya bean pie

cooking time: 12 minutes
pressure: high

you will need for 4–6 servings:

METRIC/IMPERIAL

225 g/8 oz soya beans	salt and pepper
1 (396-g/14-oz) can peeled tomatoes	450 g/1 lb potatoes, sliced
2 cloves garlic, crushed	½ teaspoon dried mixed herbs
225 g/8 oz onions, cut into eighths	75 g/3 oz cheddar cheese, grated
2 teaspoons vegetable extract	50 g/2 oz margarine or butter
1 teaspoon dried basil	3–4 tablespoons milk
2 teaspoons tomato purée	

1 Cover the soya beans with boiling water and leave to soak for 1 hour. Drain well.
2 Place beans in cooker with the trivet removed, add 300 ml/½ pint water, the tomatoes, garlic and onions. Bring to high pressure and cook for 12 minutes.
3 Reduce pressure at room temperature. Stir in vegetable extract, basil, tomato purée, salt and pepper and turn the mixture into a shallow, oven-proof dish.
4 Meanwhile, cook potatoes in boiling salted water for about 10 minutes until tender. Drain and mash with the herbs, half the cheese, margarine or butter and enough of the milk to give a soft consistency.
5 Spread over the beans, forking up the surface to give a textured appearance. Sprinkle with remaining cheese.
6 Place under a moderate grill for 10–15 minutes until heated through and lightly browned.

Variation:
Use herbs and 1 teaspoon curry powder with the potato.

Brown rice pilaff

cooking time: 18 minutes
pressure: high

you will need for 4–6 servings:

METRIC/IMPERIAL

50 g/2 oz margarine	1 tablespoon vegetable extract
350 g/12 oz onion, chopped coarsely	450 g/1 lb brown rice
225 g/8 oz celery heart, sliced	50 g/2 oz sultanas
½ teaspoon dried thyme	100 g/4 oz peanuts
½ teaspoon dried marjoram	100 g/4 oz red pepper, deseeded and sliced
1 litre/1¾ pints vegetable stock	salt and pepper

1 Melt the margarine in the cooker with the trivet removed, put in the onion, celery and herbs, cook gently for 5 minutes.

2 Remove the vegetables with a slotted spoon and put them on a plate. Pour the stock into the cooker, add the vegetable extract and stir round to dissolve.
3 Bring to the boil; stir in the rice, making sure the cooker is no more than half full. Bring to high pressure and cook for 15 minutes.
4 Reduce pressure with cold water; stir in the remaining ingredients. Return to high pressure and cook for 3 minutes.
5 Reduce pressure at room temperature. Taste and adjust seasoning. Serve with grated parmesan cheese and a tossed salad.

Kidney bean stew

cooking time: 15 minutes
pressure: high

you will need for 6–8 servings:

METRIC/IMPERIAL

175 g/6 oz yellow split peas	225 g/8 oz carrots, peeled and sliced
175 g/6 oz red kidney beans	350 g/12 oz leeks, washed and cut into 2·5-cm/ 1-inch lengths
175 g/6 oz black-eyed beans	350 g/12 oz onions, cut into eighths
1 litre/1¾ pints stock	2 cloves garlic, crushed
1 teaspoon dried mixed herbs	salt and pepper
1 tablespoon vegetable extract	

1 Place the peas and beans in a bowl, cover with cold water and leave to soak for 1 hour.
2 Drain and place in the cooker with the trivet removed, add the stock, mixed herbs and vegetable extract; stir round. Bring to high pressure and cook for 12 minutes.
3 Reduce pressure at room temperature. Stir the beans well, and add remaining ingredients. Bring to high pressure and cook for 3 minutes.
4 Reduce pressure at room temperature. Serve in a heated dish sprinkled heavily with chopped parsley and accompanied by a tossed green salad.

Kidney beans salad

cooking time: 10 minutes
pressure: high

you will need for 4 servings:

METRIC/IMPERIAL

225 g/8 oz red kidney beans	100 g/4 oz onions, finely chopped
pinch each salt, pepper, mustard, castor sugar	225 g/8 oz tomatoes, peeled and sliced
5 tablespoons sunflower oil	3 tablespoons chopped parsley
2 tablespoons white wine vinegar	salt and pepper
2–3 cloves garlic, crushed	4 eggs, hard-boiled
	sprigs of parsley

1 Cover the beans with boiling water and leave to soak for 30 minutes.
2 Drain the beans, put them in the cooker with the trivet removed and pour in 300 ml/½ pint water. Bring to high pressure and cook for 10 minutes.
3 Reduce pressure with water and drain the beans, transferring them to a bowl.
4 Place seasonings in a bowl, blend them together, add the oil and gradually stir in the vinegar. Add the garlic and chopped onions and stir the mixture into the beans. Allow to stand for 5 minutes.
5 Stir in the tomatoes and sprigs of parsley gently. Taste and adjust seasoning. Arrange on a serving dish and put in the refrigerator to chill.
6 Remove shells from the eggs and cut each into quarters; arrange on the dish and garnish with a sprig of parsley.
7 Serve with a crisp green salad and French bread.

Variation:
Instead of eggs, serve with cottage or cream cheese.

Hint:
A Meaux mustard will give extra piquancy.

Lentil and potato cake

cooking time: 7 minutes
pressure: high

you will need for 4 servings:

METRIC/IMPERIAL

225 g/8 oz red lentils, thoroughly washed	2 teaspoons vegetable extract
350 g/12 oz potatoes, peeled and sliced	½ teaspoon dried thyme
225 g/8 oz onion, chopped	100 g/4 oz hazelnuts, chopped or milled
450 ml/¾ pint water	1 large egg, beaten
salt and pepper	100 g/4 oz margarine

1 Put the lentils in the cooker with the trivet removed, add potatoes, onion, water, salt, pepper and vegetable extract, and stir. Bring to high pressure and cook for 7 minutes.
2 Reduce pressure at room temperature. Stir in the thyme, nuts and beaten egg and leave to cool a little.
3 Melt half the margarine in a large frying pan until it bubbles, carefully add the lentil mixture, level the surface with a fork and fry gently for 10 minutes or until the underneath has browned and is crisp.
4 Turn on to a plate. Melt the remaining margarine and slide the lentil cake carefully into the pan the other way up and cook the other side for a further 10 minutes.
5 Turn out and serve with parsley or onion sauce.

Variations:
a Use a strong grated cheddar cheese instead of nuts and continue as before; it may be necessary to use extra margarine for frying or even to cook it under the grill.
b Both these lentil cakes could be shaped into small cakes or rissoles, rolled in crumbs and fried.
c Serve any version with a well-flavoured tomato sauce.

Lentil and mushroom hotpot

cooking time: 12 minutes
pressure: high

you will need for 6 servings:

METRIC/IMPERIAL

1 litre/1¾ pints stock	1 tablespoon tomato purée
450 g/1 lb red lentils	salt and pepper
225 g/8 oz onions, chopped	25 g/1 oz margarine
225 g/8 oz carrots, sliced	350 g/12 oz button mushrooms, washed
2 sticks celery, washed and sliced	1 teaspoon dried basil

1 Put the stock in the cooker with the trivet removed, bring to the boil and stir in the lentils. Bring to high pressure and cook for 8 minutes.
2 Reduce pressure with cold water. Add the onions, carrots and celery and stir in the tomato purée, salt and pepper. Keep on one side.
3 Melt the margarine in a saucepan, add the mushrooms and basil and sauté for 1 minute. Stir into the cooker, return to high pressure and cook for 4 minutes.
4 Reduce pressure with cold water. Serve with a crisp tossed salad.

Rice provençale

cooking time: 5 minutes
pressure: high

you will need for 4 servings:

METRIC/IMPERIAL

2 tablespoons vegetable oil	4 tomatoes, peeled and quartered
2 onions, sliced	salt and pepper
225g/8 oz American long-grain rice	1 teaspoon dried marjoram
225 g/8 oz courgettes, sliced	2 cloves garlic, crushed
1 red pepper, sliced	600 ml/1 pint stock
1 green pepper, sliced	75 g/3 oz hard cheese, grated

1 Heat the oil in the open cooker with the trivet removed, fry the onion and rice until the rice is transparent and golden brown.

2 Add courgettes, pepper, tomatoes, season with salt and pepper, marjoram, crushed garlic. Pour in the stock, making sure the cooker is no more than half full.
3 Bring to the boil and stir once, then bring to high pressure and cook for 5 minutes.
4 Reduce pressure immediately with cold water. Serve garnished with grated Parmesan cheese.

Variations:

a If liked, add a few prawns to the rice, and chopped parsley, serve with grated parmesan cheese.
b A colourful addition would be diced salami and chopped chives sprinkled over the top.

Vegetable and nut pie

cooking time: 10 minutes
pressure: high

you will need for 6 servings:

METRIC/IMPERIAL

175 g/6 oz chick peas	¼ teaspoon ground
225 g/8 oz onions,	coriander
roughly chopped	½ teaspoon dried thyme
225 g/8 oz carrots,	2 teaspoons vegetable
scraped and thickly	extract
sliced	1 (227-g/8-oz) can peeled
225 g/8 oz celery, washed	tomatoes
and sliced	salt and pepper
175 g/6 oz peanuts,	675 g/1½ lb potatoes,
chopped	peeled and sliced
1 clove garlic, crushed	25 g/1 oz melted butter
¼ teaspoon cumin seed	

1 Cover the chick peas with boiling water and leave to stand for about 3 hours. Meanwhile, prepare the vegetables and nuts.
2 Drain the chick peas and put them in the cooker with the trivet removed with 300 ml/½ pint water. Bring to high pressure and cook for 6 minutes.
3 Reduce pressure with cold water. Add the vegetables, nuts, garlic, herbs, vegetable extract, tomatoes, salt and pepper. Return to high pressure and cook for 4 minutes.
4 Meanwhile, cook the potatoes separately in boiling salted water for 8 minutes until just tender. Drain.
5 Reduce pressure with water. Turn the vegetables and nuts into an ovenproof dish. Arrange the potatoes in a layer on top, brush them with melted butter and place them under a hot grill to lightly brown.

Variation:

Make a crumble with 150 g/5 oz wholemeal flour, 75 g/3 oz butter rubbed in and 100 g/4 oz cheese added, sprinkle it over the top of the vegetables and place under a moderate grill or in a moderately hot oven (190°C, 375°F, Gas Mark 5) for 20 minutes.

Soya bean curry

cooking time: 15 minutes
pressure: high

you will need for 4 servings:

METRIC/IMPERIAL

175 g/6 oz soya beans	2 tablespoons orange
50 g/2 oz margarine	marmalade
350 g/12 oz onions,	¼ teaspoon ground
chopped	ginger
2 cloves garlic, crushed	2 eating apples, peeled,
1 tablespoon curry powder	cored and diced in large
1 teaspoon curry paste	pieces
600 ml/1 pint stock	50 g/2 oz sultanas
1 tablespoon tomato purée	salt

1 Cover the soya beans with boiling water and leave to soak for 30 minutes. Rinse well.
2 Melt the margarine in the cooker with the trivet removed, put in the onions, garlic, curry powder and paste. Cook for 5 minutes.
3 Stir in the stock and the beans. Bring to high pressure and cook for 9 minutes.
4 Reduce pressure at room temperature. Stir in the purée, marmalade, ginger, apples and sultanas. Cover this with the trivet.
5 Put the rice in a china soufflé dish which will fit into the cooker, pour in the boiling water and a little salt, and stir. Cover with foil and tie down. Place the dish on the trivet, return to high pressure and cook for 6 minutes.
6 Reduce pressure with cold water. Remove the rice, uncover and stir then arrange it on a heated dish, add salt to the curry and serve it in the centre of the dish.
7 Serve with salted peanuts, banana, chutney, red-currant jelly and diced cucumber.

Sweets and Puddings

There are a number of puddings for which pressure cooking is ideally suited, particularly those which need long, slow cooking, such as steamed sponge puddings, sweet suet pudding, Christmas pudding, rice and other milk puddings, egg custards, dried fruits, and fresh fruits which need long cooking, for example, hard, whole pears. Other soft fruits, because of the short cooking time required, are better cooked in the conventional way.

Hints:

When making a pudding that needs covering with foil or greaseproof paper, tie it securely with string and either make a string handle or pass a foil sling under the basin for easy removal when the pudding is cooked and too hot to touch.

Make sure the correct amount of water is in the cooker. Lemon juice or vinegar added to the water helps to prevent discoloration of the cooker.

Sponge, suet and Christmas puddings should be pre-steamed before placing under pressure. This is done by covering with the lid but allowing the steam to escape through the open vent before putting on the weight, bringing slowly to the required pressure and cooking for the recommended time. Follow instructions for reducing pressure.

Marmalade sponge pudding

pre-steaming time: 25 minutes
cooking time: 25 minutes
pressure: low

you will need for 4–6 servings:

METRIC/IMPERIAL
3 tablespoons marmalade
100 g/4 oz margarine
100 g/4 oz castor sugar
2 large eggs

175 g/6 oz self-raising flour
1 orange

1 Lightly grease a 1-litre/1¾-pint pudding basin. Put the marmalade in the base.
2 Place the margarine, sugar, eggs, flour, grated orange rind and the juice of half the orange in a mixing bowl. Beat with a wooden spoon for about 2–3 minutes until well mixed and soft in texture.
3 Transfer the mixture into the prepared bowl, cover with two layers of greased greaseproof paper and tie down with string. Fill the cooker with 1 litre/1¼ pints boiling water, making sure it is no more than half full, then place the pudding on the trivet.
4 Cover with the lid, but leave off the weight; pre-steam for 25 minutes on a low heat so that the water is simmering and steam escaping from the vent.
5 Put on the weight, bring to low pressure and cook for a further 25 minutes. Allow 5–10 minutes longer if using a glass or china bowl.
6 Reduce pressure at room temperature. Turn out and serve with extra marmalade heated and served separately.

Variations:
a *Lemon:* Use lemon rind and juice instead of orange.
b *Ginger:* Use ginger marmalade and omit orange; add 1 teaspoon ground ginger to the sponge mixture.
c *Cherry:* Make a plain sponge but add 50 g/2 oz quartered glacé cherries to the mixture and replace 25 g/1 oz flour with ground almonds; also add a little almond essence. Serve with a fairly thin custard.

Pineapple upside-down pudding

pre-steaming time: 15 minutes
cooking time: 20 minutes
pressure: low

you will need for 4–6 servings:

METRIC/IMPERIAL
1 (439-g/15½-oz) can
   pineapple rings
4 glacé cherries, halved
2 tablespoons golden syrup
100 g/4 oz margarine

100 g/4 oz castor sugar
2 large eggs
150 g/6 oz self-raising flour
½ teaspoon baking powder

for sauce:
1 teaspoon cornflour

1 Drain the juice from the pineapple.
2 Well grease a 15-cm/6-inch cake tin, line the base with greaseproof paper, arrange the pineapple rings in the base and place a cherry in the centre of each. Spoon over the golden syrup.
3 Put the margarine, castor sugar, eggs, flour and baking powder in a mixing bowl, beat together with a wooden spoon for 2–3 minutes. Spread the mixture evenly over the pineapple. Cover with double greaseproof paper and foil; tie down.
4 Pour 1 litre/2 pints of water into the cooker and place the tin on the trivet. Put lid into position without the weight. Bring water slowly to simmer so steam escapes through the vent and cook for 15 minutes.
5 Put the weight on the cooker and bring to low pressure for 20 minutes.

6 Reduce pressure at room temperature. Thicken the pineapple juice and serve as a sauce.

Variations:

a Use canned apricots, mandarins or fresh stoned plums instead of pineapple.

b Add 25 g/1 oz dessicated coconut instead of the same amount of flour.

c Grated orange or lemon rind could be added to the sponge (top or bottom).

d Add 25 g/1 oz cocoa instead of same amount of flour and use with canned pears. A little more milk (2–3 tablespoons) may be needed to give a soft consistency.

● **Hints:**

a Check that the tin will fit into the cooker before making.

b Make a foil sling to go under the tin for ease of lifting in or out of cooker.

Fruit-capped puddings

pre-steaming time: 25 minutes
cooking time: 30 minutes
pressure: low

you will need for 6 servings:

METRIC/IMPERIAL

1 (396-g/14-oz) can blackcurrant pie filling	175 g/6 oz castor sugar
	3 large eggs, separated
175 g/6 oz soft margarine	175 g/6 oz self-raising flour

1 Well grease a 1·25-litre/2-pint pudding basin, put 2 tablespoons pie filling in the base.

2 Put the remaining ingredients in a bowl and beat with a wooden spoon until mixture is smooth. Spoon mixture into the basin over the pie filling, cover with double greaseproof paper and tie down with string.

3 Fill the cooker with 1 litre/1¾ pints boiling water, place a foil sling or string handle round the basin and lower it on to the trivet in the cooker.

4 Cover with the lid and pre-steam with the weight off for 25 minutes, then put the weight on, bring to low pressure and cook for a further 30 minutes, allowing an extra 5 minutes for a glass or china basin.

5 Reduce pressure at room temperature. Turn out of the basin on to a heated dish.

6 Heat the remaining pie filling and serve separately as a sauce.

Variations:

a Use other pie fillings, for example blackberry and apple with grated lemon rind in the sponge.

b Try cherry pie filling and replace 25 g/1 oz flour with the same quantity of ground almonds, also adding a few drops of almond essence.

c Apricot pie filling with grated orange rind in the sponge makes an appetizing change.

Apricot duchess pudding

cooking time: 20 minutes
pressure: high

you will need for 6 servings:

METRIC/IMPERIAL

450 ml/¾ pint milk	25 g/1 oz butter
3 eggs, separated	3 tablespoons apricot jam
200 g/7 oz castor sugar	25 g/1 oz flaked almonds, toasted
rind of 1 lemon, finely grated	
100 g/4 oz fresh white breadcrumbs	

1 Butter a 1·25-litre/2-pint soufflé dish. Blend the egg yolks and sugar together, stir in the lemon rind and the milk, slightly warmed, breadcrumbs and butter. Pour into the dish, cover with a double layer of greaseproof paper and tie down.

2 Put 300 ml/½ pint water into the cooker, tie a foil sling or string handle round the dish for lifting it out and place the dish on the trivet. Bring to high pressure and cook for 10 minutes.

3 Reduce pressure at room temperature. Remove the greaseproof paper, spread the pudding with the jam and sprinkle with half of the nuts.

4 Whisk the egg whites until stiff and gradually whisk in the castor sugar, a teaspoonful at a time. Fold in the remainder when the mixture gets too stiff to whisk.

5 Spread over the top of the jam, sprinkle with the remaining nuts. Cook in a preheated moderately hot oven (200°C, 400°F, Gas Mark 6) for 10 minutes, until the top is golden.

Sultana sponge with butterscotch sauce

pre-steaming time: 15 minutes
cooking time: 20 minutes
pressure: low

you will need for 4 servings:

METRIC/IMPERIAL

100 g/4 oz butter, softened	2 eggs, well beaten
	175 g/6 oz self-raising flour
100 g/4 oz soft brown sugar	75 g/3 oz sultanas
	3 tablespoons milk

for sauce:

75 g/3 oz butter	150 ml/¼ pint double cream
175 g/6 oz soft brown sugar	

1 Grease a 1-litre/1½-pint metal ring mould.

2 Cream butter and sugar together until light and creamy. Gradually beat in the eggs and fold in the flour, sultanas and milk.

3 Spread mixture evenly in the tin. Cover with double greaseproof paper and tie down.

4 Place trivet in the cooker with 1 litre/1½ pints water and put the tin on the trivet. Cover with the lid and pre-steam the pudding without the weight for 15 minutes, then put on the weight and bring to low pressure: cook for 20 minutes.

5 Reduce pressure at room temperature and turn out on to a heated dish.

6 Melt the butter for the sauce, add sugar and dissolve over a low heat.

7 Add the cream and bring to the boil. Remove from the heat immediately and serve with the pudding.

Mincemeat layer pudding

pre-steaming time: 15 minutes
cooking time: 40 minutes
pressure: low

you will need for 6 servings:

METRIC/IMPERIAL
100 g/4 oz plain flour	75 g/3 oz castor sugar
1½ teaspoons baking powder	1 egg, well beaten
¼ teaspoon salt	8 tablespoons milk
100 g/4 oz fresh white breadcrumbs	grated rind of 1 orange
75 g/3 oz prepared shredded suet	450 g/1 lb mincemeat

for sauce:
2 teaspoons cornflour	juice of 1 orange
150 ml/¼ pint water	4 tablespoons medium sherry
2 tablespoons sugar	

1 Grease a 1·5-litre/2½-pint pudding basin.

2 Sift flour, baking powder and salt into a bowl: stir in breadcrumbs, suet and sugar. Blend eggs, milk and orange rind together and mix into flour to give a soft consistency.

3 Place one-third of the mincemeat in the basin and cover with one-third of the pudding mixture. Repeat these layers twice more, then cover with double greaseproof paper or foil with a pleat in it and tie down.

4 Put the trivet in the cooker with 1 litre/1¾ pints water. Place a sling of foil under the basin, or tie a string handle round it, and place the basin on the trivet.

5 Cover with the lid but leave off the weight. Pre-steam for 15 minutes on a low heat so that the water is simmering and steam escaping from the vent.

6 Put on the weight, bring to low pressure and cook for 40 minutes, allowing an extra 5–10 minutes if a glass or china basin is used. Reduce pressure at room temperature.

7 Meanwhile, make the sauce. Blend the cornflour and water together in a pan, add the sugar and orange juice. Bring to the boil and cook for 3 minutes, add sherry and reheat.

8 Turn the pudding out on to a heated dish and serve the sauce separately.

Tangy chocolate pudding with chocolate sauce

pre-steaming time: 25 minutes
cooking time: 25 minutes
pressure: low

you will need for 4–6 servings:

METRIC/IMPERIAL
100 g/4 oz margarine	1–2 tablespoons milk
100 g/4 oz soft brown sugar	
25 g/1 oz cocoa powder	*for sauce:*
1 tablespoon hot water	100 g/4 oz soft brown sugar
2 eggs, beaten	50 g/2 oz cocoa powder
175 g/6 oz self-raising flour	150 ml/¼ pint water
grated rind of 1 orange	juice of 1 orange
	25 g/1 oz butter

to decorate:
1 orange, sliced

1 Beat margarine and sugar together until light and creamy. Blend cocoa powder with hot water and beat into mixture.

2 Gradually add eggs, beating well between each addition. Fold in flour and orange rind. Stir in sufficient milk to give a dropping consistency.

3 Turn mixture into a greased 1-litre/1½-pint pudding basin and cover with double layer greased greaseproof paper or foil. Tie down, making a foil sling or string handle for lifting.

4 Put 1 litre/1¾ pints boiling water in the cooker and stand the basin on the trivet. Pre-steam with the vent open for 25 minutes, then put on the weight and bring to low pressure. Cook for 25 minutes. Reduce pressure at room temperature.

5 Meanwhile, to make the sauce put all the ingredients in a saucepan. Heat slowly and stir until sugar has dissolved, then boil rapidly for 2–3 minutes until sauce coats the back of a wooden spoon.

6 Turn pudding out on to a warmed serving dish and decorate with halved slices of orange round the edge of the dish. Spoon a little chocolate sauce on top of pudding and serve the rest separately. Serve hot.

To freeze:

7 Make pudding in the normal way and cook. Cool, remove pudding from the basin and wrap in greased heavy duty foil. Alternatively, cook the pudding in a foil basin. Cool, seal and freeze. Storage time; up to 3 months.

To thaw:

8 Remove foil and replace frozen pudding in greased basin, or if in a foil basin leave it there to reheat. Cover top with greased foil and pre-steam with vent open for 30 minutes to thaw and reheat. Make sauce as required.

Nutty chocolate pudding

pre-steaming time: 25 minutes
cooking time: 25 minutes
pressure: low

you will need for 4–6 servings:

METRIC/IMPERIAL

6 tablespoons chocolate spread	100 g/4 oz castor sugar
15 g/½ oz butter or margarine	25 g/1 oz dessicated coconut
2 teaspoons milk	75 g/3 oz self-raising flour
2 large eggs	25 g/1 oz cocoa powder
100 g/4 oz soft margarine	½ teaspoon vanilla essence

1 Put the chocolate spread, butter and milk in a small saucepan, heat gently to blend together. Pour into a lightly greased 1·25-litre/2-pint pudding basin.
2 Place the remaining ingredients in a bowl and beat together for 2 minutes. Spoon into the basin, mix well, cover with a double piece of greaseproof paper and foil and tie down.
3 Fill cooker with 1 litre/1¾ pints boiling water, place pudding basin on the trivet with a foil sling or string handle round it.
4 Cover with the lid, but leave off the weight: pre-steam on a low heat so that the water is simmering and steam escaping from the vent for 25 minutes.
5 Put on the weight, bring to low pressure and cook for 25 minutes. Allow 5–10 minutes longer if using a glass or china basin.
6 Reduce pressure at room temperature. Turn out and serve at once.

Apple and currant roly-poly

pre-steaming time: 10 minutes
cooking time: 25 minutes
pressure: low

you will need for 4–6 servings:

METRIC/IMPERIAL

100 g/4 oz self-raising flour	75 g/3 oz shredded suet
50 g/2 oz fresh white breadcrumbs	pinch salt
	cold water to mix

for filling:

1 cooking apple, peeled, cored and chopped	2 tablespoons soft brown sugar
1 tablespoon currants	

1 Put the flour, crumbs, suet and salt in a bowl. Mix to a soft but not sticky dough with cold water. Roll out on a lightly floured surface into an oblong not more than 18 cm/7 inches wide.
2 Mix filling ingredients together and spread out evenly over the dough. Damp pastry edges with water.
3 Roll up from the short side and seal ends well together. Wrap in a floured cloth lined with greaseproof or non-stick paper.

4 Bring 900 ml/1½ pints water with 1 tablespoon lemon juice to the boil in the cooker and place the pudding on the trivet. Put the lid on the cooker and with the vent open steam for 10 minutes without pressure.
5 Bring to low pressure in the usual way and cook for 25 minutes. Reduce pressure at room temperature.
6 Lift out pudding, unwrap on to a warmed serving dish. Serve with whipped cream or custard.

Lemon sunshine pudding

pre-steaming time: 5 minutes
cooking time: 10 minutes
pressure: high

you will need for 4 servings:

METRIC/IMPERIAL

100 g/4 oz fresh white breadcrumbs	grated rind and juice of 1 lemon
50 g/2 oz Atora suet	1 egg, beaten
100 g/4 oz castor sugar	

for sauce (optional):

4 tablespoons lemon curd	15 g/½ oz sugar
2 teaspoons lemon juice	small knob butter

1 Mix together the breadcrumbs, suet and sugar. Add lemon rind and juice and egg, mixing thoroughly.
2 Transfer mixture into four individual-sized 200-ml/7-fl oz plastic or foil pudding basins. Cover securely with lid, foil or double greaseproof paper and tie down with string, making a handle of foil or string for lifting.
3 Fill the cooker with 600 ml/1 pint water: place the puddings on the trivet. With the vent open, pre-steam for 5 minutes, then put the weight on and bring to high pressure and cook for 10 minutes.
4 Reduce pressure at room temperature. Turn out the puddings on to a warmed serving dish.

Variation:
If liked, a lemon sauce could be served with this pudding; mix together the lemon curd, lemon juice, sugar and knob of butter. Heat through and serve separately.

Banana pudding with lemon sauce

pre-steaming time: 15 minutes
cooking time: 25 minutes
pressure: low

you will need for 4–6 servings:

METRIC/IMPERIAL

100 g/4 oz butter or margarine	grated rind of 1 lemon
100 g/4 oz castor sugar	100 g/4 oz self-raising flour
2 eggs, well beaten	2 ripe bananas, sliced

for sauce:

1 tablespoon custard powder	juice of 1 lemon
300 ml/½ pint water	25 g/1 oz castor sugar

1 Cream butter and sugar together until light and fluffy. Gradually beat in the eggs. Fold in the lemon rind and flour, stir in the bananas.
2 Well grease a 1-litre/1½-pint pudding basin and spoon in the mixture. Cover with a double layer of greaseproof paper with a pleat in it and tie down securely with string.
3 Pour 1 litre/1¾ pints water into the cooker. Place a foil sling or string handle round the basin and lift it on to the trivet in the cooker.
4 Pre-steam with the lid on but without the weight for 15 minutes. Put on the weight, bring to low pressure and cook for 25 minutes. Reduce pressure at room temperature.
5 Meanwhile, make the sauce by blending the custard powder with a little of the water: add the lemon juice. Heat gently in a small saucepan, stirring: bring to the boil and cook until sauce thickens. Stir in sugar.
6 Turn pudding out of the basin and serve the sauce separately.

Variation:
Dried banana could also be used – use 100 g/4 oz thinly sliced.

Orange and date pudding

pre-steaming time: 10 minutes
cooking time: 30 minutes
pressure: high

you will need for 4–6 servings:

METRIC/IMPERIAL
75 g/3 oz self-raising flour
75 g/3 oz fresh white breadcrumbs
75 g/3 oz prepared beef suet
75 g/3 oz demerara sugar
50 g/2 oz dates, chopped
grated rind and juice of 2 oranges
1 large egg, well beaten

1 Mix the flour, breadcrumbs, suet, sugar and dates together. Stir in the grated rind, orange juice and egg. Mix well.
2 Lightly grease a 1-litre/1½-pint pudding basin, put in the mixture and level the surface. Cover with a double layer of greaseproof paper. Tie down with string, making a handle from string or foil to aid lifting.
3 Put 1 litre/1¾ pints water in the cooker and stand the bowl on the trivet. Pre-steam with the vent open for 10 minutes.
4 Put on the weight, bring to high pressure and cook for 30 minutes.
5 Reduce pressure at room temperature. Turn the pudding out on to a warmed dish and serve with custard.

Variations:
a Try it with chopped dried apricots instead of the dates.
b Mixed dried fruit in place of the dates would make an interesting variation.
c Dried banana instead of dates would be delicious.
d Chopped preserved ginger and a ½ teaspoon ground ginger could be added. Leave out the orange rind and juice, but add 3 tablespoons milk.

Lemon pudding

pre-steaming time: 10 minutes
cooking time: 50 minutes
pressure: high

you will need for 4 servings:

METRIC/IMPERIAL
50 g/2 oz plain flour
pinch salt
1 teaspoon baking powder
100 g/4 oz sugar
100 g/4 oz finely chopped suet
225 g/8 oz breadcrumbs
grated rind and juice of 2 lemons
2 eggs
200 ml/7 fl oz milk

1 Grease a 1-litre/1¾-pint basin. Sift the flour, salt and baking powder and add the sugar, suet, breadcrumbs and lemon rind.
2 Stir in well-beaten eggs and lemon juice, adding milk as required to make a dropping consistency. The amount of milk depends on the size of the lemons.
3 Pour mixture into the basin, cover with greaseproof paper and tie down, making a handle from string or foil to aid lifting.
4 Pour 1 litre/1¾ pints water into the cooker and stand the pudding on the trivet. Pre-steam with the lid on but without the weight for 10 minutes.
5 Put on the weight and bring to high pressure. Cook for 50 minutes.
6 Reduce pressure at room temperature. Turn the pudding out on to a warmed dish.

Variation:
Use oranges instead of lemons. Again, the amount of milk required will depend on the size of the oranges.

Cinnamon pudding

pre-steaming time: 15 minutes
cooking time: 30 minutes
pressure: high

you will need for 4 servings:
METRIC/IMPERIAL
75 g/3 oz brown sugar
75 g/3 oz margarine
100 g/4 oz self-raising flour
1 teaspoon baking powder
1 tablespoon cinnamon
pinch salt
1 egg
100 g/4 oz breadcrumbs
75 g/3 oz sultanas
milk to mix

1 Cream together the sugar and margarine. Sift

together the flour, baking powder, cinnamon and salt. Beat in the egg.

2 Fold alternately breadcrumbs and flour mix into the creamed mixture. Fold in sultanas and add enough milk to give a dropping consistency.

3 Place the mixture in a 1-litre/1¾-pint pudding basin, cover with double greaseproof paper and tie down, making a foil or string handle to aid lifting. Pre-steam for 15 minutes with the lid on but without the weight.

4 Put on the weight, bring to high pressure and cook for 30 minutes. Reduce pressure at room temperature.

5 Turn the pudding out on to a warmed dish. Serve with a lemon sauce or with custard.

Roly poly

pre-steaming time: 10 minutes
cooking time: 20 minutes
pressure: high

you will need for 6 servings:

METRIC/IMPERIAL
350 g/12 oz plain flour	pinch salt
2 round teaspoons baking powder	water to mix
	jam
175 g/6 oz prepared suet	

1 Sift the flour and baking powder, add the suet and salt. Mix with sufficient water to make a soft but firm dough. Roll it into a rectangle 5 mm/¼ inch thick.

2 Spread with jam almost to the edge. Damp the edges and roll the pastry up. Seal the edges and wrap the pudding in a cloth or greased greaseproof paper or foil. Seal or tie up the ends of the wrapping.

3 Fill cooker with 1 litre/1¾ pints water, place the wrapped pudding on the trivet. Cover with the lid but without the weight and pre-steam for 10 minutes.

4 Put on the weight and bring to high pressure. Cook for 20 minutes. Reduce pressure at room temperature. Remove pudding from wrapping and serve extra jam sauce if required.

Variations:

a **Spotted Dick:** Sprinkle 175 g/6 oz mixed fruit over the suet pastry.

b Serve plain with golden syrup poured over.

c Spread pastry with 2 tablespoons ginger marmalade, sprinkle with 75 g/3 oz glacé cherries and 50 g/2 oz seedless raisins. Serve with a ginger marmalade, golden syrup or lemon sauce.

⬤ Hints:

a Always add lemon or vinegar to water to stop discoloration.

b Make sure there is always enough water: as a guide, allow 150 ml/¼ pint for every 15 minutes cooking time, plus 300 ml/½ pint for steaming time.

Spiced rhubarb pudding

pre-steaming time: 15 minutes
cooking time: 30 minutes
pressure: high

you will need for 6 servings:

METRIC/IMPERIAL
225 g/8 oz plain flour	450 g/1 lb rhubarb
75–100 g/3–4 oz prepared suet	50 g/2 oz sultanas
	50 g/2 oz currants
1 teaspoon baking powder	50 g/2 oz raisins
¼ teaspoon salt	50 g/2 oz brown sugar
cold water to mix	1 teaspoon mixed spice

1 Sift flour, salt and baking powder and mix in suet. Mix to a firm dough with cold water. Grease a 1-litre/1¾-pint pudding basin.

2 Clean fruit, cut rhubarb into pieces about 1 cm/½ inch in length and mix with dried fruit, sugar and spices.

3 Divide suet crust into 3 portions and use one piece for the base of the basin; cover it with half the rhubarb mixture. Roll out the second piece and put it on top, add the remainder of the rhubarb mixture.

4 Cover with the third piece of rolled-out crust. Cover with double greaseproof paper and tie it down, making a foil or string handle for easy lifting.

5 Put 1 litre/1¾ pints water in the cooker and place the bowl on the trivet. Cover with the lid but leave the vent open, and pre-steam for 15 minutes.

6 Put on the weight and bring to high pressure. Cook for 30 minutes. Reduce pressure at room temperature.

7 Turn out on to a warmed dish. Serve with cream or custard.

Fruit suet

pre-steaming time: 15 minutes
cooking time: 35 minutes
pressure: high

you will need for 4–6 servings:

METRIC/IMPERIAL
225 g/8 oz plain flour	675 g/1½ lb fresh fruit,
75–100 g/3–4 oz suet	sweetened to taste
1 teaspoon baking powder	(rhubarb, apple,
¼ teaspoon salt	blackberry, etc)
cold water to mix	

1 Sift flour, salt and baking powder. Mix in suet to a firm dough with water. Cut off one-third of the dough, roll out the remainder and use it to line a greased 1-litre/1¾-pint basin.

2 Fill the basin with selected fruit and, unless the fruit is juicy, 1 tablespoon water, and a sprinkling of sugar.

3 Roll out the remaining piece of pastry and cover the fruit. Cover the basin with a double piece of grease-proof paper and tie it down, making a string or foil handle to aid lifting.

4 Put 1 litre/1¾ pints water in the cooker and place the bowl on the trivet. Cover with the lid but without the weight and pre-steam for 15 minutes.
5 Put on the weight, bring to high pressure and cook for 35 minutes. Reduce pressure at room temperature.

Gloucester pudding

pre-steaming time: 15 minutes
cooking time: 55 minutes
pressure: high

you will need for 6 servings:

METRIC/IMPERIAL

100 g/4 oz self-raising flour	50 g/2 oz castor sugar
100 g/4 oz suet	50 g/2 oz ground rice
100 g/4 oz dried mixed fruit	1 egg, beaten
	150 ml/¼ pint milk

1 Mix all the ingredients together. Lightly grease a 1-litre/1¾-pint basin and put the mixture into it.
2 Cover with a double layer of foil and tie down, making a handle of string or foil to aid lifting.
3 Fill the cooker with 1 litre/1¾ pints water, stand the basin on the trivet, cover with the lid but without the weight and pre-steam for 15 minutes.
4 Put on the weight, bring to high pressure and cook for 55 minutes.
Reduce pressure at room temperature.

Toffee apple pudding

pre-steaming time: 15 minutes
cooking time: 30 minutes
pressure: low

you will need for 4–6 servings:

METRIC/IMPERIAL

little butter	8 tablespoons milk
25 g/1 oz dark soft brown sugar	*for filling:*
225 g/8 oz self-raising flour	450 g/1 lb cooking apples, peeled, cored and thinly sliced
100 g/4 oz prepared suet	50 g/2 oz dark soft brown sugar
½ teaspoon ground cinnamon	

1 Lightly butter a 1-litre/1¾-pint pudding basin, press 25 g/1 oz dark soft brown sugar on the base and sides.
2 Mix together flour, suet and cinnamon with about 8 tablespoons milk to give a soft dough. Roll out two thirds of the dough and use it to line the basin.
3 Mix together the apples and sugar and fill the basin.

Roll out the remaining piece of dough, damp the top edges of the suet pastry with cold water and cover the pudding.
4 Make a pleat in a double piece of greaseproof paper, cover the pudding and tie it down with string, forming a handle out of string or foil to aid lifting.
5 Pour 1 litre/1¾ pints water into the cooker and stand the basin on the trivet. Cover with the lid but leave the vent open and pre-steam for 15 minutes. Put on the weight, bring to low pressure and cook for 30 minutes.
6 Reduce pressure at room temperature.

Variations:
a Add coarsely grated orange or lemon rind to the apples.
b A few raisins with the apple and a few cloves would make a nice change.

Bread and butter pudding

cooking time: 6 minutes
pressure: high

you will need for 4 servings:

METRIC/IMPERIAL

6 slices white bread, buttered	150 ml/¼ pint milk
50 g/2 oz castor sugar	150 ml/¼ pint single cream
50 g/2 oz currants	3 eggs, lightly beaten
50 g/2 oz sultanas	300 ml/½ pint water
pinch cinnamon	1 tablespoon demerara sugar

1 Butter an ovenproof dish which can be accommodated in your cooker and will fit under the grill. Remove the crusts from the buttered bread and cut each slice into quarters.
2 Arrange the bread, sugar, currants and sultanas in layers in the dish, sprinkling with cinnamon. Heat the milk and cream to blood heat and pour over the lightly beaten eggs. Strain over the bread mixture.
3 Cover the dish with foil or a double layer of greased greaseproof paper and tie under the rim, making a handle out of foil or string.
4 Pour the water into the cooker and stand the pudding on the trivet. Bring to high pressure and cook for 6 minutes.
5 Allow the pressure to reduce at room temperature. Lift out the pudding, take off the paper, sprinkle the surface with demerara sugar and brown lightly under a moderate grill.

Variations:
a Use mincemeat in the layers instead of the dried fruit but spread the slices with less butter.
b Spread with lemon curd and add grated lemon rind to the egg mixture.
c Spread the bread with orange marmalade. Cook as before. Put a meringue topping on and cook in a low oven to crisp.

Cabinet pudding

cooking time: 10 minutes
pressure: high

you will need for 6 servings:

METRIC/IMPERIAL
100 g/4 oz stoned raisins
225 g/8 oz bread
4 eggs
25 g/1 oz sugar
600 ml/1 pint milk
vanilla essence

1 Grease a 1-litre/1¾-pint pudding basin and decorate the base and sides with a few halved raisins. Cut the bread into slices, then into 1-cm/1½-inch squares and beat the eggs.
2 Warm the milk, stir in sugar and pour on to the beaten eggs. Add vanilla essence to taste. Add bread and remaining raisins and soak for ½ hour.
3 Pour the mixture into the basin, cover with double greaseproof paper and tie down, making a foil or string handle to aid lifting.
4 Fill the cooker with 600 ml/1 pint water and place the bowl on the trivet. Bring to high pressure and cook for 10 minutes.
5 Reduce pressure at room temperature.

Variations:

a Serve with raspberry or apricot sauce made from jam melted and strained, thinned down with lemon juice to make it less sweet.
b Instead of vanilla essence, infuse the milk with strips of lemon peel.
c If liked, sponge trifle cakes could be used instead of bread; they would not need much soaking. Also add a dash of sherry.

● **Hint:**
Ready-sliced bread will not need a long soak because the bread is softer to start with.

Milk puddings

cooking time: 7–12 minutes
pressure: medium

you will need for 4 servings:

METRIC/IMPERIAL
25 g/1 oz butter or
 margarine
50 g/2 oz cereal (rice,
 semolina, sago, etc.)
40 g/1½ oz sugar
600 ml/1 pint milk

1 Melt the butter or margarine in the open cooker, pour in the milk and bring it to the boil; add cereal and sugar and stir well.
2 Lower heat to simmering point, put on cover and bring to medium pressure. Cook rice or barley for 12 minutes and tapioca, sago or semolina for 7 minutes.
3 Reduce pressure at room temperature. Put into a serving dish, sprinkle with nutmeg and brown under a hot grill.

Variations:

a Vanilla, lemon rind or orange rind may be added.
b To rice, add chopped dried apricots at the beginning of the cooking time.
c When cooked rice has cooled, fold in 300 ml/½ pint whipped double cream and pile into individual glass dishes. Top with grated chocolate and serve chilled.
d Add fresh fruits to cooked semolina to give it a bite; chopped apples, pears, or other fruit.
e Add 1 tablespoon cocoa or drinking chocolate to the warmed milk before pouring over sago for a chocolate flavour.
f Add porridge oats, chopped nuts, mixed dried fruits and fresh chopped fruit to cooled puddings to bulk out the rice and make a summer meusli.

Egg custard

cooking time: 5 minutes
pressure: high

you will need for 4 servings:

METRIC/IMPERIAL
2 eggs
50 g/2 oz sugar
450 ml/¾ pint milk

1 Beat together eggs and sugar. Warm the milk, pour on to the eggs and sugar and beat well.
2 Pour into 0·75-litre/1-pint china or heatproof glass dish which has been well greased and cover with greaseproof paper or foil.
3 Put 300 ml/½ pint water into the cooker with a little lemon juice or vinegar. Place the dish on the trivet, bring to high pressure and cook for 5 minutes.
4 Reduce pressure at room temperature and serve either hot or cold.

Variations:

Caramel custard: Make caramel with 75 g/3 oz loaf sugar and 4 tablespoons water. Heat the sugar and water together, stir until the sugar dissolves, remove spoon and allow to boil until the liquid is golden brown. Pour the caramel into a warm heatproof glass or china dish and proceed with custard as for egg custard. Serve cold.

Crème brûlée

cooking time: 10 minutes
pressure: high

you will need for 4–6 servings:

METRIC/IMPERIAL
450 ml/¾ pint milk
150 ml/¼ pint double
 cream
75 g/3 oz castor sugar
4 large eggs
1 teaspoon vanilla essence
100 g/4 oz demerara sugar

1 Put the milk, cream and castor sugar in a saucepan and heat gently to dissolve the sugar.

2 Break the eggs into a mixing bowl, add the vanilla and whisk lightly. Stir in the warm milk, then strain into a straight-sided 1·25-litre/2-pint soufflé dish.

3 Cover with foil or a double layer of greaseproof paper and tie down, making a foil or string handle to aid lifting. Put 300 ml/½ pint water in the cooker and place the dish on the trivet. Bring to high pressure and cook for 10 minutes.

4 Reduce pressure at room temperature. Lift out and allow to set at room temperature, then chill well.

5 Sprinkle top with the remaining sugar, place under a preheated hot grill and cook until the sugar begins to melt.

Hint:
It is important to cover the top securely.

Festive orange pudding with sherry sauce

pre-steaming time: 10 minutes
cooking time: 65 minutes
pressure: high

you will need for 4 servings:

METRIC/IMPERIAL	
1 large orange	75 g/3 oz plain flour
75 g/3 oz stoneless dates	50 g/2 oz soft brown sugar
1 cooking apple, peeled and cored	75 g/3 oz shredded suet
	75 g/3 oz seedless raisins
1 large carrot, peeled	¼ teaspoon mixed spice
65 g/2½ oz fresh white breadcrumbs	pinch salt
	1 egg, beaten

for sauce:

1 orange	2 tablespoons medium sherry
½ tablespoon arrowroot	
25 g/1 oz sugar	

1 Pare rind from the orange, cut into thin strips and reserve.

2 Remove pith and pips and finely mince the orange flesh, dates, apples and carrots. Alternatively, finely chop the orange flesh and dates and grate the apples and carrot.

3 Mix together the breadcrumbs, flour, sugar, suet, raisins, mixed spice, salt and orange rind and stir into the orange mixture. Beat the egg and add.

4 Turn into a well-greased 1-litre/1½-pint pudding basin, cover with double greaseproof paper and tie down, making a foil or string handle to hold it by.

5 Fill the cooker with 1 litre/1¾ pints water, and place the pudding on the trivet. Cover with the lid and pre-steam without the weight for 10 minutes, then put on the weight, bring to high pressure and cook for 65 minutes.

6 Meanwhile, make the sauce. Grate rind from the orange and reserve. Squeeze the orange and make up juice to 300 ml/½ pint with water. Heat in a saucepan and bring to the boil.

7 Blend arrowroot and sugar with 2 tablespoons water and pour on the orange juice. Return to pan with the sherry added and bring to the boil, stirring until the sauce thickens and clears.

8 Reduce pressure at room temperature. Turn out the pudding on to a warmed serving dish and serve with the sauce.

Mother's Christmas pudding

pre-steaming time: 20 minutes
cooking time: 2 hours
pressure: high

you will need for 2 (675-g/1½-lb) puddings:

METRIC/IMPERIAL	
175 g/6 oz fresh or prepared suet	50 g/2 oz plain flour
	100 g/4 oz mixed peel
100 g/4 oz currants	100 g/4 oz demerara sugar
½ teaspoon mixed spice	rind of ½ lemon and ½ orange
350 g/12 oz seedless raisins	
	50 g/2 oz ground almonds
175 g/6 oz fresh breadcrumbs	½ teaspoon salt
	3 tablespoons brandy
150 ml/¼ pint Guinness	3 eggs, well beaten

1 If using fresh suet, grate it. Mix all the ingredients together and divide between two 1·5-litre/2½-pint pudding basins.

2 Cover with double greaseproof paper and tie down with string, forming a handle out of string or foil for easy lifting.

3 Cook one pudding at a time; fill the cooker with 1·75 litres/3 pints water. Place the pudding on the trivet; cover with the lid and pre-steam for 20 minutes without the weight.

4 Put on the weight, bring to high pressure and cook for 2½ hours. Reduce pressure at room temperature.

5 Allow to cool. Remove covering, then cover with clean greaseproof and foil or a square of calico tied at the corners. Store in a cool, dry place, or freeze until required.

6 To reheat, return the pudding to the cooker and bring to high pressure according to the following chart:

General guide to cooking and reheating Christmas Puddings:

Weight up to:	Water	pre-steaming	cooking at pressure	Reheating
450 g/ 1 lb	1·25 litres/ 2¼ pints	20 minutes	1¾ hours	20 minutes
675 g/ 1½ lb	1·75 litres /3 pints	20 minutes	2½ hours	30 minutes
1 kg/ 2 lb	2 litres/ 3½ pints	30 minutes	3 hours	30 minutes

7 Reduce pressure at room temperature, turn out the pudding on to a warmed dish and serve with brandy butter, cream, custard, or a sweet white sauce.

Honey pudding

pre-steaming time: 10 minutes
cooking time: 35 minutes
pressure: high

you will need for 4 servings:

METRIC/IMPERIAL

4 teaspoons clear honey	75 g/3 oz butter or
175 g/6 oz flour	margarine
pinch salt	50 g/2 oz sugar
1 rounded teaspoon	1 egg
baking powder	milk to mix

1 Grease a 1-litre/1¾-pint pudding basin and put 2 teaspoons of honey in the bottom of it.
2 Sift together the flour, salt and baking powder. Rub in butter or margarine and add the sugar. Beat together the egg and remaining honey and stir into the dry ingredients with enough milk to make a dropping consistency.
3 Put the mixture into the pudding basin, cover with a double layer of greaseproof paper and tie down, making a foil or string handle to aid lifting.
4 Put 1 litre/1¾ pints water in the cooker with a little vinegar, place the pudding on the trivet, cover with the lid and with the vent open pre-steam for 10 minutes.
5 Put on the weight, bring to high pressure and cook for 35 minutes. Reduce pressure at room temperature.

Gingerbread pudding

pre-steaming time: 10 minutes
cooking time: 50 minutes
pressure: high

you will need for 4–6 servings:

METRIC/IMPERIAL

225 g/8 oz plain flour	225 g/8 oz golden syrup
pinch salt	1 egg
1 teaspoon baking powder	milk to mix
1 teaspoon ground ginger	
100 g/4 oz finely chopped	
suet	

1 Grease a 1-litre/1¾-pint mould or basin.
2 Sift together flour, salt, baking powder and ginger and mix with the suet. Warm syrup, beat together syrup, egg and a little milk. Stir this into the dry ingredients, mixing well.
3 If necessary, add more milk to give a dropping consistency; pour into the prepared basin, cover with double greaseproof paper and tie down, making a string or foil handle to aid lifting.
4 Put 1 litre/1¾ pints water in the cooker, adding vinegar or lemon juice. Place the basin on the trivet. cover with the lid but without the weight, and pre-steam for 10 minutes.

5 Put on the weight, bring to high pressure and cook for 50 minutes.
6 Reduce pressure at room temperature.

Rhubarb and orange compote

cooking time: nil
pressure: medium

you will need for 4–6 servings:

METRIC/IMPERIAL

450 g/1 lb frozen rhubarb	grated rind and juice of
150 ml/¼ pint water	1 orange
175 g/6 oz granulated	1 tablespoon arrowroot
sugar	

1 Put the frozen rhubarb in the cooker with the trivet removed. Pour in the water, sugar and grated orange rind.
2 Bring up to medium pressure slowly, then switch off the heat and reduce pressure at room temperature.
3 Remove the rhubarb with a slotted spoon, draining it well, and transfer it to a glass serving dish or individual dishes.
4 Blend the arrowroot with the squeezed orange juice. Stir into the juice in the cooker and bring to the boil, stirring; reduce heat and simmer for 2 minutes for the arrowroot to clear.
5 Pour over the fruit and allow it to cool before serving.

Variations:

a Try adding grated lemon rind and juice instead of orange with ½ teaspoon ground ginger.
b Cook the rhubarb with ginger ale.
c Cook with a dilution of blackcurrant juice.
d Serve the compote on top of a layer of canned rice. This will give about 8 helpings.

● **Hint:**
To keep the rhubarb in whole pieces, it is important to bring it slowly to pressure.

Prune compote

cooking time: 10 minutes
pressure: high

you will need for 4 servings:

METRIC/IMPERIAL

225 g/8 oz dried prunes	1 tablespoon undiluted
rind of ½ lemon	orange squash
300 ml/½ pint weak tea	40 g/1½ oz demerara sugar

1 Cover the prunes with boiling water and leave to soak for 15 minutes.
2 Place the lemon rind, tea, squash and sugar in the

cooker with the trivet removed. Heat to dissolve the sugar. Drain the prunes and add them to the cooker.

3 Bring to high pressure and cook for 10 minutes. Reduce pressure at room temperature.

4 Lift out the prunes with a slotted spoon into a serving dish. Reduce the liquid until it becomes syrupy, then pour it over the fruit.

Variations:

a Use ginger ale instead of tea; make up the quantity with water.

b If available, use a spiced evening tea (a special blend of tea) to give a different flavour.

Hint:

If preferred, prunes can be soaked overnight. It is then only necessary to cook them for 5 minutes at high pressure.

Bananas with lemon sauce

cooking time: nil
pressure: high

you will need for 3–4 servings:

METRIC/IMPERIAL

15 g/½ oz butter	I tablespoon patent
50 g/2 oz soft brown	cornflour
sugar	juice of I lemon
pinch ground nutmeg or	water as required
cinnamon	4 firm bananas, peeled
grated rind of I lemon	

1 Place the butter, sugar, nutmeg, lemon rind and cornflour in the cooker with the trivet removed.

2 Make up the lemon juice to 150 ml/¼ pint with water and stir into the cooker. Bring to the boil, stirring all the time.

3 Add the bananas, bring to high pressure and then reduce pressure immediately with cold water.

4 Serve with whipped cream if liked.

Cranapples

cooking time: 4 minutes
pressure: high

you will need for 4 servings:

METRIC/IMPERIAL

4 large cooking apples	grated rind of ½ lemon
I (170-g/6-oz) jar	pinch ground cloves
Cranberry sauce	150 ml/¼ pint water
3 tablespoons brown sugar	

1 Wash the apples and remove the core. Make a slit in the skin all round the centre.

2 Mix together the cranberry sauce, brown sugar,

lemon and cloves and use to stuff the apples.

3 Pour the water into the cooker and stand the apples on the trivet. Bring to high pressure and cook for 4 minutes.

4 Reduce pressure with cold water.

Pears in cider

cooking time: 4–8 minutes
pressure: high

you will need for 4 servings:

METRIC/IMPERIAL

4 cooking pears	15 g/½ oz butter
150 ml/¼ pint sweet cider	rind and juice of I orange
150 ml/¼ pint water	2 tablespoons golden syrup
50 g/2 oz demerara sugar	

1 Peel the pears and leave whole with the stalks on.

2 Place the remaining ingredients in the cooker with the trivet removed. Heat gently to dissolve the sugar, then put back the trivet and place the pears on top.

3 Cover, bring to high pressure and cook for 4–8 minutes depending on how hard the pears are.

4 Reduce pressure at room temperature. Transfer the pears to a serving dish.

5 Reduce the liquor until it becomes syrupy. Spoon it over the pears and serve either hot or cold with ice cream.

Variations:

a Replace cider with all water and use honey instead of golden syrup with lemon rind and juice.

b If liked, add a few chopped glacé fruits to the sauce.

c Use ginger ale for all the liquid and stir in some chopped ginger at the end.

d Use orange juice and rind in larger amounts and add some orange segments to the sauce just before serving.

● **Hint:**

The success of this dish is dependent on all the pears being in the same condition so that they cook evenly.

Chutneys and preserves

With the revival of interest in home-grown produce, there is a great advantage in using a pressure cooker to make a range of preserves for the store cupboard.

Remembering that the cooker must never be more than half filled and the cooking time is short, several small batches can be made, giving a wider choice with less wastage. Using a pressure cooker for this purpose reduces the time involved considerably.

I have created a range of different chutneys and jams which I hope will become family favourites.

Green tomato chutney

cooking time: 8 minutes
pressure: high

you will need for 1·5 kg/3 lb chutney:

METRIC/IMPERIAL

675 g/1½ lb green tomatoes, chopped
225 g/8 oz cooking apples, chopped
½ cucumber, cubed
225 g/8 oz onions, sliced
300 ml/½ pint vinegar
50 g/2 oz sultanas

1 teaspoon salt
2 cloves garlic
1 teaspoon ground ginger
1 teaspoon dry mustard
¼ teaspoon cayenne pepper
350 g/12 oz demerara sugar

1 Put the tomatoes, apples, cucumber, onions, vinegar, sultanas, salt and garlic in the cooker with the trivet removed. Bring to high pressure and cook for 8 minutes.
2 Reduce pressure at room temperature. Stir in remaining ingredients, heat gently until the sugar has dissolved, then boil fairly fast until mixture is fairly thick.
3 Pour into warmed jars, cover with thin polythene, seal and label.

Tomato and apple chutney

cooking time: 10 minutes
pressure: high

you will need for 1·5 kg/3 lb:

METRIC/IMPERIAL

1 kg/2 lb red or green tomatoes
225 g/8 oz onions
450 g/1 lb cooking apples
2 cloves garlic, crushed

450 ml/¾ pint malt vinegar
1 teaspoon salt
450 g/1 lb demerara sugar
½ teaspoon ground ginger

1 Chop the tomatoes and onions, peel and slice apples.
2 Put them all in the cooker with the trivet removed and add the garlic, vinegar and salt. Bring to high pressure and cook for 10 minutes.
3 Reduce pressure at room temperature. Stir in the sugar, heating gently to dissolve.
4 Bring to the boil and cook fairly rapidly to reduce the chutney, about 15 minutes.
5 Stir in the ginger, then pour into clean, warmed jars. Cover with thin polythene, seal and label.

Variation:
Stir in 15 g/½ oz mustard seed instead of the ginger.

Apple chutney

cooking time: 10 minutes
pressure: high

you will need for 1·5 kg/3 lb chutney:

METRIC/IMPERIAL

1·25 kg/2½ lb cooking apples
450 ml/¾ pint vinegar
350 g/12 oz demerara sugar

15 g/½ oz salt
15 g/½ oz mustard seed
15 g/½ oz ground ginger
1 clove garlic, crushed
½ teaspoon cayenne pepper

1 Peel and thickly slice the apples, put them in the cooker with the trivet removed and add 300 ml/½ pint vinegar. Bring to high pressure and cook for 10 minutes.
2 Reduce pressure at room temperature. Add the remaining ingredients, bring to the boil, stirring to dissolve the sugar and simmer for 10 minutes to reduce and thicken.
3 Pour into a bowl and leave covered for 1 week, stirring occasionally.
4 Put into clean jars, seal and label.

Tomato and date chutney

cooking time: 8 minutes
pressure: high

you will need for 1·75 kg/4 lb chutney:

METRIC/IMPERIAL

1 kg/2 lb green and red tomatoes, cut up roughly
350 g/12 oz cooking apples, cored and chopped
225 g/8 oz onions, chopped
300 ml/½ pint malt vinegar

1 teaspoon salt
1–2 cloves garlic, crushed (optional)
1 teaspoon crushed chillies
350 g/12 oz demerara sugar
225 g/8 oz chopped dates

1 Put the tomatoes, apples, onions, vinegar, salt, garlic and chillies in the cooker with the trivet removed, making sure the cooker is no more than half full. Bring to high pressure and cook for 8 minutes.
2 Reduce pressure at room temperature. Stir in the sugar and chopped dates, boil gently for about 20 minutes until the chutney is thick.
3 Pour into clean warmed jars, cover with thin polythene and label. Leave to mature for about 1 month.

Variations:
a Use sultanas instead of dates.
b Leave out crushed chillies and add ½ teaspoon cayenne pepper and ½ teaspoon ground ginger.

1 Wash the plums and remove the stones, put the plums in the cooker with the trivet removed and add the apples, onions, dates, sultanas, lemon juice, salt, nutmeg, chillies and bay leaves.
2 Stir in 300 ml/½ pint vinegar, making sure the cooker is no more than half full. Bring to high pressure and cook for 8 minutes.
3 Reduce pressure at room temperature, add the remaining vinegar and sugar and the marmalade. Bring to the boil, reduce heat and simmer for about 10–15 minutes, stirring frequently until the chutney is quite thick.
4 Remove bay leaves, pour into clean warmed jars with thin polythene and screw tops. Label and leave to become cold.

Beetroot chutney

cooking time: 10 minutes
pressure: high

you will need for 1·75 kg/4 lb chutney:

METRIC/IMPERIAL	
1 kg/2 lb cooked beetroot, chopped	450 ml/¾ pint malt vinegar
450 g/1 lb onions, chopped	1 teaspoon ground ginger
225 g/8 oz cooking apples, chopped	1 teaspoon dry mustard
grated rind and juice of 2 oranges	½ teaspoon cayenne pepper
	1 teaspoon salt
	450 g/1 lb granulated sugar

1 Place the beetroot, onion, apple, orange rind and juice, 300 ml/½ pint vinegar, spices and salt in the cooker with trivet removed, making sure it is no more than half full. Bring to high pressure and cook for 10 minutes.
2 Reduce pressure at room temperature. Stir in the remaining vinegar and sugar. Bring to the boil and simmer, stirring frequently until the chutney is thick, about 10–15 minutes.
3 Pour into clean warmed jars, cover with thin polythene and screw tops. Label and leave them to become cold.

Gooseberry chutney

cooking time: 10 minutes
pressure: high

you will need for 2 kg/4½ lb chutney:

METRIC/IMPERIAL	
1·5 kg/3 lb gooseberries	450 ml/¾ pint light spiced vinegar
225 g/8 oz onions, quartered	450 g/1 lb granulated sugar
225 g/8 oz dried apricots	225 g/8 oz soft brown sugar
1 tablespoon salt	
25 g/1 oz mustard seed	

1 Wash, top and tail the gooseberries, then put them through a mincer with the onions and dried apricots.
2 Put these ingredients in the cooker with the trivet removed with the salt, mustard seed and 300 ml/½ pint vinegar. Make sure the cooker is no more than half full. Bring to high pressure and cook for 10 minutes.
3 Reduce pressure at room temperature. Stir in the remaining vinegar and the sugars.
4 Bring to the boil and simmer for about 10–15 minutes, stirring frequently until the chutney is thick.
5 Pour into clean warmed jars, cover with thin polythene and screw tops. Label and leave to become cold.

Plum chutney

cooking time: 8 minutes
pressure: high

you will need for 2·25 kg/5 lb chutney:

METRIC/IMPERIAL	
1 kg/2¼ lb red plums	¼ teaspoon ground nutmeg
450 g/1 lb cooking apples, peeled and chopped	1 teaspoon crushed chillies
100 g/4 oz onions, chopped	3 bay leaves
175 g/6 oz stoned dates, chopped	450 ml/¾ pint malt vinegar
100 g/4 oz sultanas	1 kg/2 lb demerara sugar
juice of 1 lemon	4 tablespoons orange marmalade
1½ tablespoons salt	

Mango chutney

cooking time: 10 minutes
pressure: high

you will need for 1·5 kg/3 lb chutney:

METRIC/IMPERIAL	
1·5 kg/3 lb fresh mangoes or peaches	1 tablespoon pickling spice
350 g/12 oz onions, thinly sliced	1 teaspoon salt
350 g/12 oz cooking apples, peeled and sliced	350 g/12 oz soft brown sugar
450 ml/¾ pint malt vinegar	¼ teaspoon cayenne pepper

1 Using a sharp knife, cut the tough outer skin from the mangoes and cut the flesh from the stone in thin slices.
2 Put it in the open cooker with the trivet removed with the onions, apples and 300 ml/½ pint vinegar. Make sure the cooker is no more than half full.
3 Wrap the pickling spice in a double piece of muslin or a piece of old teatowel, tie together with string and place it in the cooker. Bring to high pressure and cook for 10 minutes.
4 Reduce pressure at room temperature, add the remaining vinegar, salt and sugar. Stir round to dissolve, then bring to the boil and cook gently until the chutney is quite thick.
5 Remove the muslin bag of spices and add cayenne pepper if a hotter chutney is preferred.
6 Pour into clean warmed jars, cover with thin polythene and screw tops. Label and leave to become cold.

Orange marmalade

cooking time: 10 minutes
pressure: medium

you will need for 3 kg/6½ lb marmalade:

METRIC/IMPERIAL

I kg/2 lb Seville oranges	1·75 kg/4 lb granulated
6 tablespoons lemon juice	sugar
I litre/2 pints water	

1 Wash the fruit, peel the rind thinly. Peel off the pith. Cut the fruit upon a plate. Tie pips and pith in muslin, cut the rind into thin shreds.
2 Place the cut-up fruit, juice, rind, pith and pips, lemon juice and half the water in the cooker with the trivet removed, making sure the cooker is no more than half full. Bring to medium pressure and cook for 10 minutes.
3 Reduce pressure, remove the lid and transfer the contents to a preserving pan or a large saucepan, taking out the muslin bag and squeezing it well. Add the remaining water and sugar.
4 Place the open pan over a gentle heat and stir until the sugar is dissolved. Bring to the boil and boil rapidly until setting point is reached. This can be tested by placing a little of the marmalade on a saucer. When cool, the surface should wrinkle when pushed with a finger. Remove the pan from the heat while testing.
5 Allow to stand for 15 minutes, remove scum and pour into clean warm jars. Cover with waxed paper circles and tops. Seal, label and store in a cool, dry, dark cupboard.

Three fruits ginger marmalade

cooking time: 15 minutes
pressure: medium

you will need for 2·75 kg/6 lb marmalade:

METRIC/IMPERIAL

2 oranges, I grapefruit and 2 lemons, to weigh I kg/2¼ lb	5-cm/2-inch piece dried whole ginger
750 ml/1¼ pints water	1·75 kg/4 lb preserving sugar

1 Scrub the fruit, cut in half and place in pressure cooker with half the water and the crushed ginger, making sure the cooker is no more than half full. Bring to medium pressure and cook for 15 minutes.
2 Reduce pressure at room temperature. Lift out the fruit and cut it into thin slices, using a knife and fork, discarding any pips and the ginger. Return the sliced fruit to a preserving pan or large saucepan and add the remaining water and the sugar.
3 Place the open pan over a gentle heat and stir till sugar has dissolved, then bring to the boil and boil rapidly until setting point is reached. This will take 5–20 minutes.
4 Remove pan from the heat while testing for set. Setting point is reached when a teaspoon of the mixture, cooled on a cold plate, crinkles when pushed with a finger.
5 Cool the marmalade for 5 minutes, then remove scum. Pot in warm, dry jars, cover with waxed paper circles and tops.
6 Cool, wipe jars, label and store in a cool, dry, dark cupboard.

Apricot and orange marmalade

cooking time: 10 minutes
pressure: high

you will need for 2·75 kg/6 lb marmalade:

METRIC/IMPERIAL

I kg/2 lb Seville oranges	1·75 litres/3 pints water
2 large lemons	1·75 kg/4 lb sugar
350 g/12 oz dried apricots coarsely chopped	

1 Wash the oranges and lemons, cut into quarters. Remove and keep the pips, tie them in a piece of muslin.
2 Place the fruit with 1 litre/2 pints of the water and the bag of pips in the cooker with the trivet removed. Bring to high pressure and cook for 10 minutes.
3 Reduce the pressure at room temperature. Remove the pips and squeeze out the bag, take out the fruit, allow to cool a little and mince.
4 Return to a preserving pan or a large saucepan with the remaining water and sugar. Heat gently in the open pan to dissolve the sugar, then boil rapidly for about 15–20 minutes until setting point is reached. Remove from heat while testing.

Test for setting by putting 1 teaspoon of the mixture on a cold plate. When cool, the surface should wrinkle when pushed with a finger.

Allow to stand for 15 minutes before potting; remove scum, pour into clean, warm jars. Cover with waxed paper circles and tops; seal, label and store in a cool, dry, dark cupboard.

Blackberry and apple jam

cooking time: 7 minutes
pressure: medium

you will need for 2·75 kg/6 lb jam:

METRIC/IMPERIAL
350 g/12 oz prepared cooking apples
1 kg/2 lb blackberries
150 ml/¼ pint water
1·5 kg/3 lb preserving sugar

Place the prepared apples and blackberries and water in the cooker with the trivet removed, making sure it is no more than half full. Bring to medium pressure and cook for 7 minutes.

Reduce the pressure at room temperature. Add the sugar and stir until dissolved; if necessary heat gently to dissolve, but do not boil.

When the sugar has dissolved, bring to the boil in the open cooker, and allow to cook fairly fast for 10–15 minutes or until setting point is reached. Remove from heat while testing for set.

To test for setting, put 1 teaspoon of the mixture on a cold plate. When cool, the surface should wrinkle when pushed with the finger.

Allow the jam to settle for a few minutes, then remove scum. Pour into clean, warm jars and cover with waxed paper circles and tops. Seal, label and store in a cool, dry, dark cupboard.

Hints:

A good cooking apple or an under-ripe apple will give a better setting result than those apples which can be used for either eating or cooking.

It is important to use the sugar stated in the recipes as this would have been the type of sugar used for testing the recipe originally.

Apple cinnamon jam

cooking time: 5 minutes
pressure: medium

you will need for 1·75 kg/4 lb jam:

METRIC/IMPERIAL
1·5 kg/3 lb cooking apples
1 large lemon
2½ teaspoons ground cinnamon
300 ml/½ pint water
1·5 kg/3 lb granulated sugar

1 Peel, core and cut apples into quarters. Place cores and peel in a muslin bag and tie it securely.
2 Put apples, rind and juice of the lemon, cinnamon, water and muslin bag into the pressure cooker with the trivet removed. Bring very slowly to medium pressure and cook for 5 minutes.
3 Reduce pressure at room temperature. Remove the muslin bag. Add sugar and, over a gentle heat, stir until thoroughly dissolved, then boil rapidly in the open cooker until setting point is reached. Remove from heat and test for set.
4 To test for setting, put 1 teaspoon of the mixture on a cold plate. When cool, the surface should wrinkle when pushed with the finger.
5 Allow the jam to settle for a few minutes, then re-remove scum. Pour into clean, warm jars and cover with waxed paper circles and tops. Seal, label and store in a cool, dry, dark cupboard.

Lemon curd

cooking time: 10 minutes
pressure: high

you will need for 450 g/1 lb curd:

METRIC/IMPERIAL
2 eggs
225 g/8 oz granulated sugar
50 g/2 oz butter
2 lemons

1 Beat eggs well in heatproof glass or china bowl. Add the butter cut into small pieces, the sugar and grated rind and juice of the lemons. Stir together well.
2 Cover the bowl with foil or greaseproof paper. Tie it on well, making a string or foil handle to aid lifting.
3 Put 300 ml/½ pint water into the pressure cooker and stand the basin on the trivet. Bring to high pressure and cook for 10 minutes.
4 Reduce pressure at room temperature. Stir the curd thoroughly, pour into warm dry jars and cover with waxed discs. Tie down, label and store in a cool, dry, dark cupboard.

Plum jam

cooking time: 5 minutes
pressure: medium

you will need for 2·25 kg/5 lb jam:

METRIC/IMPERIAL
1·5 kg/3 lb plums or damsons
150 ml/¼ pint water
1·5 kg/3½ lb sugar

1 Wash and stone the fruit. Retain some of the kernels from the stones.
2 Put the fruit, water and blanched kernels into the

pressure cooker with the trivet removed. Bring to high pressure and cook for 5 minutes.

3 Reduce pressure at room temperature. Add the sugar and stir over gentle heat until dissolved.

4 Boil rapidly in open cooker until setting point is reached. This should take about 10–15 minutes. Remove from heat and test for set.

5 To test for setting, put 1 teaspoon of the mixture on a cold plate. When cool, the surface should wrinkle when pushed with the finger.

6 Allow the jam to settle for a few minutes, then skim with a metal spoon. Pour into clean, warm jars and cover with waxed paper circles and tops. Seal, label and store in a cool, dry, dark cupboard.

2 Reduce pressure at room temperature. Add the sugar and lemon juice and stir until the sugar is dissolved. Add walnuts if used.

3 Return the cooker to the heat, bring to the boil and boil for about 10–15 minutes until setting point is reached. Remove from heat and test for set.

4 To test for setting, put 1 teaspoon of the mixture on a cold plate. When cool, the surface should wrinkle when pushed with the finger.

5 Allow the jam to settle for a few minutes, then remove scum with a metal spoon. Pour into clean, warm jars and cover with waxed paper circles and tops. Seal, label and store in a cool, dry, dark cupboard.

Mixed fruit jam

cooking time: 3 minutes
pressure: medium

you will need for 1·5–1·75 kg/3–4 lb jam:

METRIC/IMPERIAL
250 g/8 oz strawberries	150 g/5 oz cherries
150 g/5 oz gooseberries	75 g/3 oz blackcurrants
150 g/5 oz greengages	1 kg/2 lb granulated sugar
150 g/5 oz raspberries	300 ml/$\frac{1}{2}$ pint water

1 Prepare, stone and wash the fruit. Put it into the cooker with the trivet removed and add the water. Bring to medium pressure and cook for 3 minutes.

2 Reduce pressure at room temperature. Stir in the sugar, cook gently until it has dissolved, then bring to the boil rapidly and boil for about 25 minutes until setting point is reached. Remove from heat and test for set.

3 To test for setting, put 1 teaspoon of the mixture on a cold plate. When cool, the surface should wrinkle when pushed with the finger.

4 Allow the jam to settle for a few minutes, then remove scum. Pour into clean, warm jars and cover with waxed paper circles and tops. Seal, label and store in a cool, dry, dark cupboard.

Dried apricot jam

cooking time: 10 minutes
pressure: high

you will need for 2·25 kg/5 lb jam:

METRIC/IMPERIAL
450 g/1 lb dried apricots	juice of 1 large lemon
900 ml/1$\frac{1}{2}$ pints water	halved walnuts (optional)
1·5 kg/3 lb sugar	

1 Wash the dried fruit and boil the water. Put the fruit into the cooker with the trivet removed and pour over it the boiling water. Leave to soak for 5–10 minutes, then bring to high pressure and cook for 10 minutes.

Index